BOURBON TASTING

LOGBOOK

THIS BELONGS TO

PHONE	EMAIL
START DATE	LAST DATE

CONTENTS

CONTENTS

BOURBON LOG

BOURBON NAME	DATE TASTED

PRODUCER	DISTILLERY

TYPE / GRADE	COUNTRY OF ORIGIN

STILL TYPE	REGION

AGE	ALCOHOL %	PRICE	BOTTLE SIZE

QUALITY RATING

1	2	3	4	5	6	7	8	9	10

VALUE FOR MONEY

1	2	3	4	5	6	7	8	9	10

COLOR METER

- BLACK
- DARK BROWN
- MAHOGANY
- BRICK
- DARK AMBER
- AMBER
- GOLD
- STRAW
- CLEAR

FLAVOR WHEEL

BALANCE
HEAT / ABM _____ %
FINISH
FRESH FRUIT
BODY
DARK FRUIT
PEATY / SMOKY
CITRUS FRUIT
SHARP / ACIDIC
DRIED FRUIT
ASTRINGENT
HERBAL / VEGETAL
ROASTED / WOODY
SPICES
MOLASSES
SWEET / CANDIED

FLAVOR NOTES

SMELL / SCENT NOTES

OTHER NOTES

BOURBON NAME		DATE TASTED

PRODUCER	DISTILLERY

TYPE / GRADE	COUNTRY OF ORIGIN

STILL TYPE	REGION

AGE	ALCOHOL %	PRICE	BOTTLE SIZE

QUALITY RATING

1	2	3	4	5	6	7	8	9	10

VALUE FOR MONEY

1	2	3	4	5	6	7	8	9	10

COLOR METER

BLACK
DARK BROWN
MAHOGANY
BRICK
DARK AMBER
AMBER
GOLD
STRAW
CLEAR

FLAVOR WHEEL

BALANCE, FINISH, BODY, PEATY / SMOKY, SHARP / ACIDIC, ASTRINGENT, ROASTED / WOODY, MOLASSES, SWEET / CANDIED, SPICES, HERBAL / VEGETAL, DRIED FRUIT, CITRUS FRUIT, DARK FRUIT, FRESH FRUIT, HEAT / ABM _____ %

FLAVOR NOTES

SMELL / SCENT NOTES

OTHER NOTES

BOURBON LOG

BOURBON NAME	DATE TASTED

PRODUCER	DISTILLERY

TYPE / GRADE	COUNTRY OF ORIGIN

STILL TYPE	REGION

AGE	ALCOHOL %	PRICE	BOTTLE SIZE

QUALITY RATING	VALUE FOR MONEY
1 2 3 4 5 6 7 8 9 10	1 2 3 4 5 6 7 8 9 10

COLOR METER

- BLACK
- DARK BROWN
- MAHOGANY
- BRICK
- DARK AMBER
- AMBER
- GOLD
- STRAW
- CLEAR

FLAVOR WHEEL

HEAT / ABM _____ %

BALANCE
FINISH
BODY
FRESH FRUIT
PEATY / SMOKY
DARK FRUIT
SHARP / ACIDIC
CITRUS FRUIT
ASTRINGENT
DRIED FRUIT
ROASTED / WOODY
HERBAL / VEGETAL
MOLASSES
SPICES
SWEET / CANDIED

FLAVOR NOTES

SMELL / SCENT NOTES	OTHER NOTES

BOURBON NAME		DATE TASTED
PRODUCER	DISTILLERY	
TYPE / GRADE	COUNTRY OF ORIGIN	
STILL TYPE	REGION	

AGE	ALCOHOL %	PRICE	BOTTLE SIZE

QUALITY RATING

1	2	3	4	5	6	7	8	9	10

VALUE FOR MONEY

1	2	3	4	5	6	7	8	9	10

COLOR METER

- BLACK
- DARK BROWN
- MAHOGANY
- BRICK
- DARK AMBER
- AMBER
- GOLD
- STRAW
- CLEAR

FLAVOR WHEEL

BALANCE HEAT / ABM _____ %
FINISH FRESH FRUIT
BODY DARK FRUIT
PEATY / SMOKY CITRUS FRUIT
SHARP / ACIDIC DRIED FRUIT
ASTRINGENT HERBAL / VEGETAL
ROASTED / WOODY SPICES
MOLASSES SWEET / CANDIED

FLAVOR NOTES

SMELL / SCENT NOTES

OTHER NOTES

BOURBON LOG

BOURBON NAME	DATE TASTED

PRODUCER	DISTILLERY

TYPE / GRADE	COUNTRY OF ORIGIN

STILL TYPE	REGION

AGE	ALCOHOL %	PRICE	BOTTLE SIZE

QUALITY RATING

1	2	3	4	5	6	7	8	9	10

VALUE FOR MONEY

1	2	3	4	5	6	7	8	9	10

COLOR METER

- BLACK
- DARK BROWN
- MAHOGANY
- BRICK
- DARK AMBER
- AMBER
- GOLD
- STRAW
- CLEAR

FLAVOR WHEEL

HEAT / ABM _____ %

BALANCE
FINISH
BODY
PEATY / SMOKY
SHARP / ACIDIC
ASTRINGENT
ROASTED / WOODY
MOLASSES
SWEET / CANDIED
SPICES
HERBAL / VEGETAL
DRIED FRUIT
CITRUS FRUIT
DARK FRUIT
FRESH FRUIT

FLAVOR NOTES

SMELL / SCENT NOTES

OTHER NOTES

8

BOURBON NAME		DATE TASTED	

PRODUCER	DISTILLERY

TYPE / GRADE	COUNTRY OF ORIGIN

STILL TYPE	REGION

AGE	ALCOHOL %	PRICE	BOTTLE SIZE

QUALITY RATING

1	2	3	4	5	6	7	8	9	10

VALUE FOR MONEY

1	2	3	4	5	6	7	8	9	10

COLOR METER

- BLACK
- DARK BROWN
- MAHOGANY
- BRICK
- DARK AMBER
- AMBER
- GOLD
- STRAW
- CLEAR

FLAVOR WHEEL

HEAT / ABM _____ %

BALANCE, FINISH, BODY, PEATY / SMOKY, SHARP / ACIDIC, ASTRINGENT, ROASTED / WOODY, MOLASSES, SWEET / CANDIED, SPICES, HERBAL / VEGETAL, DRIED FRUIT, CITRUS FRUIT, DARK FRUIT, FRESH FRUIT

FLAVOR NOTES

SMELL / SCENT NOTES	OTHER NOTES

BOURBON LOG

BOURBON NAME		DATE TASTED

PRODUCER	DISTILLERY

TYPE / GRADE	COUNTRY OF ORIGIN

STILL TYPE	REGION

AGE	ALCOHOL %	PRICE	BOTTLE SIZE

QUALITY RATING

1	2	3	4	5	6	7	8	9	10

VALUE FOR MONEY

1	2	3	4	5	6	7	8	9	10

COLOR METER	FLAVOR WHEEL	FLAVOR NOTES

COLOR METER

- BLACK
- DARK BROWN
- MAHOGANY
- BRICK
- DARK AMBER
- AMBER
- GOLD
- STRAW
- CLEAR

FLAVOR WHEEL

HEAT / ABM _____ %

BALANCE
FINISH
BODY
PEATY / SMOKY
SHARP / ACIDIC
ASTRINGENT
ROASTED / WOODY
MOLASSES
SWEET / CANDIED
SPICES
HERBAL / VEGETAL
DRIED FRUIT
CITRUS FRUIT
DARK FRUIT
FRESH FRUIT

FLAVOR NOTES

SMELL / SCENT NOTES	OTHER NOTES

BOURBON NAME	DATE TASTED

PRODUCER	DISTILLERY

TYPE / GRADE	COUNTRY OF ORIGIN

STILL TYPE	REGION

AGE	ALCOHOL %	PRICE	BOTTLE SIZE

QUALITY RATING

1	2	3	4	5	6	7	8	9	10

VALUE FOR MONEY

1	2	3	4	5	6	7	8	9	10

COLOR METER

- BLACK
- DARK BROWN
- MAHOGANY
- BRICK
- DARK AMBER
- AMBER
- GOLD
- STRAW
- CLEAR

FLAVOR WHEEL

HEAT / ABM _____ %

BALANCE
FINISH
BODY
PEATY / SMOKY
SHARP / ACIDIC
ASTRINGENT
ROASTED / WOODY
MOLASSES
SWEET / CANDIED
SPICES
HERBAL / VEGETAL
DRIED FRUIT
CITRUS FRUIT
DARK FRUIT
FRESH FRUIT

FLAVOR NOTES

SMELL / SCENT NOTES

OTHER NOTES

BOURBON LOG

BOURBON NAME	DATE TASTED

PRODUCER	DISTILLERY

TYPE / GRADE	COUNTRY OF ORIGIN

STILL TYPE	REGION

AGE	ALCOHOL %	PRICE	BOTTLE SIZE

QUALITY RATING

1	2	3	4	5	6	7	8	9	10

VALUE FOR MONEY

1	2	3	4	5	6	7	8	9	10

COLOR METER

- BLACK
- DARK BROWN
- MAHOGANY
- BRICK
- DARK AMBER
- AMBER
- GOLD
- STRAW
- CLEAR

FLAVOR WHEEL

HEAT / ABM _____ %

BALANCE
FINISH
BODY
PEATY / SMOKY
SHARP / ACIDIC
ASTRINGENT
ROASTED / WOODY
MOLASSES
SWEET / CANDIED
SPICES
HERBAL / VEGETAL
DRIED FRUIT
CITRUS FRUIT
DARK FRUIT
FRESH FRUIT

FLAVOR NOTES

SMELL / SCENT NOTES

OTHER NOTES

BOURBON NAME		DATE TASTED

PRODUCER	DISTILLERY

TYPE / GRADE	COUNTRY OF ORIGIN

STILL TYPE	REGION

AGE	ALCOHOL %	PRICE	BOTTLE SIZE

QUALITY RATING

1	2	3	4	5	6	7	8	9	10

VALUE FOR MONEY

1	2	3	4	5	6	7	8	9	10

COLOR METER

- BLACK
- DARK BROWN
- MAHOGANY
- BRICK
- DARK AMBER
- AMBER
- GOLD
- STRAW
- CLEAR

FLAVOR WHEEL

BALANCE HEAT / ABM _____ %
FINISH FRESH FRUIT
BODY DARK FRUIT
PEATY / SMOKY CITRUS FRUIT
SHARP / ACIDIC DRIED FRUIT
ASTRINGENT HERBAL / VEGETAL
ROASTED / WOODY SPICES
MOLASSES SWEET / CANDIED

FLAVOR NOTES

SMELL / SCENT NOTES

OTHER NOTES

13

BOURBON LOG

BOURBON NAME	DATE TASTED

PRODUCER	DISTILLERY

TYPE / GRADE	COUNTRY OF ORIGIN

STILL TYPE	REGION

AGE	ALCOHOL %	PRICE	BOTTLE SIZE

QUALITY RATING

1	2	3	4	5	6	7	8	9	10

VALUE FOR MONEY

1	2	3	4	5	6	7	8	9	10

COLOR METER

- BLACK
- DARK BROWN
- MAHOGANY
- BRICK
- DARK AMBER
- AMBER
- GOLD
- STRAW
- CLEAR

FLAVOR WHEEL

HEAT / ABM _____ %

BALANCE

FINISH

BODY

FRESH FRUIT

PEATY / SMOKY

DARK FRUIT

SHARP / ACIDIC

CITRUS FRUIT

ASTRINGENT

DRIED FRUIT

ROASTED / WOODY

HERBAL / VEGETAL

MOLASSES

SPICES

SWEET / CANDIED

FLAVOR NOTES

SMELL / SCENT NOTES

OTHER NOTES

BOURBON NAME	DATE TASTED

PRODUCER	DISTILLERY

TYPE / GRADE	COUNTRY OF ORIGIN

STILL TYPE	REGION

AGE	ALCOHOL %	PRICE	BOTTLE SIZE

QUALITY RATING

1	2	3	4	5	6	7	8	9	10

VALUE FOR MONEY

1	2	3	4	5	6	7	8	9	10

COLOR METER

- BLACK
- DARK BROWN
- MAHOGANY
- BRICK
- DARK AMBER
- AMBER
- GOLD
- STRAW
- CLEAR

FLAVOR WHEEL

HEAT / ABM _____ %

BALANCE, FINISH, BODY, PEATY / SMOKY, SHARP / ACIDIC, ASTRINGENT, ROASTED / WOODY, MOLASSES, SWEET / CANDIED, SPICES, HERBAL / VEGETAL, DRIED FRUIT, CITRUS FRUIT, DARK FRUIT, FRESH FRUIT

FLAVOR NOTES

SMELL / SCENT NOTES

OTHER NOTES

BOURBON LOG

BOURBON NAME	DATE TASTED

PRODUCER	DISTILLERY

TYPE / GRADE	COUNTRY OF ORIGIN

STILL TYPE	REGION

AGE	ALCOHOL %	PRICE	BOTTLE SIZE

QUALITY RATING	VALUE FOR MONEY
1 2 3 4 5 6 7 8 9 10	1 2 3 4 5 6 7 8 9 10

COLOR METER

- BLACK
- DARK BROWN
- MAHOGANY
- BRICK
- DARK AMBER
- AMBER
- GOLD
- STRAW
- CLEAR

FLAVOR WHEEL

HEAT / ABM _____ %

BALANCE
FINISH
BODY
PEATY / SMOKY
SHARP / ACIDIC
ASTRINGENT
ROASTED / WOODY
MOLASSES
SWEET / CANDIED
SPICES
HERBAL / VEGETAL
DRIED FRUIT
CITRUS FRUIT
DARK FRUIT
FRESH FRUIT

FLAVOR NOTES

SMELL / SCENT NOTES

OTHER NOTES

BOURBON NAME		DATE TASTED

PRODUCER	DISTILLERY

TYPE / GRADE	COUNTRY OF ORIGIN

STILL TYPE	REGION

AGE	ALCOHOL %	PRICE	BOTTLE SIZE

QUALITY RATING

1	2	3	4	5	6	7	8	9	10

VALUE FOR MONEY

1	2	3	4	5	6	7	8	9	10

COLOR METER

BLACK
DARK BROWN
MAHOGANY
BRICK
DARK AMBER
AMBER
GOLD
STRAW
CLEAR

FLAVOR WHEEL

BALANCE, FINISH, BODY, PEATY / SMOKY, SHARP / ACIDIC, ASTRINGENT, ROASTED / WOODY, MOLASSES, SWEET / CANDIED, SPICES, HERBAL / VEGETAL, DRIED FRUIT, CITRUS FRUIT, DARK FRUIT, FRESH FRUIT, HEAT / ABM _____ %

FLAVOR NOTES

SMELL / SCENT NOTES

OTHER NOTES

BOURBON LOG

BOURBON NAME	DATE TASTED

PRODUCER	DISTILLERY

TYPE / GRADE	COUNTRY OF ORIGIN

STILL TYPE	REGION

AGE	ALCOHOL %	PRICE	BOTTLE SIZE

QUALITY RATING

1	2	3	4	5	6	7	8	9	10

VALUE FOR MONEY

1	2	3	4	5	6	7	8	9	10

COLOR METER

- BLACK
- DARK BROWN
- MAHOGANY
- BRICK
- DARK AMBER
- AMBER
- GOLD
- STRAW
- CLEAR

FLAVOR WHEEL

HEAT / ABM _____ %

BALANCE
FINISH
BODY
PEATY / SMOKY
SHARP / ACIDIC
ASTRINGENT
ROASTED / WOODY
MOLASSES
SWEET / CANDIED
SPICES
HERBAL / VEGETAL
DRIED FRUIT
CITRUS FRUIT
DARK FRUIT
FRESH FRUIT

FLAVOR NOTES

SMELL / SCENT NOTES

OTHER NOTES

BOURBON NAME		DATE TASTED

PRODUCER	DISTILLERY

TYPE / GRADE	COUNTRY OF ORIGIN

STILL TYPE	REGION

AGE	ALCOHOL %	PRICE	BOTTLE SIZE

QUALITY RATING

1	2	3	4	5	6	7	8	9	10

VALUE FOR MONEY

1	2	3	4	5	6	7	8	9	10

COLOR METER

- BLACK
- DARK BROWN
- MAHOGANY
- BRICK
- DARK AMBER
- AMBER
- GOLD
- STRAW
- CLEAR

FLAVOR WHEEL

BALANCE, FINISH, BODY, PEATY / SMOKY, SHARP / ACIDIC, ASTRINGENT, ROASTED / WOODY, MOLASSES, SWEET / CANDIED, SPICES, HERBAL / VEGETAL, DRIED FRUIT, CITRUS FRUIT, DARK FRUIT, FRESH FRUIT, HEAT / ABM _____ %

FLAVOR NOTES

SMELL / SCENT NOTES

OTHER NOTES

BOURBON LOG

BOURBON NAME	DATE TASTED

PRODUCER	DISTILLERY

TYPE / GRADE	COUNTRY OF ORIGIN

STILL TYPE	REGION

AGE	ALCOHOL %	PRICE	BOTTLE SIZE

QUALITY RATING

1	2	3	4	5	6	7	8	9	10

VALUE FOR MONEY

1	2	3	4	5	6	7	8	9	10

COLOR METER

- BLACK
- DARK BROWN
- MAHOGANY
- BRICK
- DARK AMBER
- AMBER
- GOLD
- STRAW
- CLEAR

FLAVOR WHEEL

HEAT / ABM _____ %

BALANCE
FINISH
BODY
PEATY / SMOKY
SHARP / ACIDIC
ASTRINGENT
ROASTED / WOODY
MOLASSES
SWEET / CANDIED
SPICES
HERBAL / VEGETAL
DRIED FRUIT
CITRUS FRUIT
DARK FRUIT
FRESH FRUIT

FLAVOR NOTES

SMELL / SCENT NOTES

OTHER NOTES

BOURBON NAME	DATE TASTED

PRODUCER	DISTILLERY

TYPE / GRADE	COUNTRY OF ORIGIN

STILL TYPE	REGION

AGE	ALCOHOL %	PRICE	BOTTLE SIZE

QUALITY RATING

1	2	3	4	5	6	7	8	9	10

VALUE FOR MONEY

1	2	3	4	5	6	7	8	9	10

COLOR METER

- BLACK
- DARK BROWN
- MAHOGANY
- BRICK
- DARK AMBER
- AMBER
- GOLD
- STRAW
- CLEAR

FLAVOR WHEEL

BALANCE · HEAT / ABM _____ %
FINISH · FRESH FRUIT
BODY · DARK FRUIT
PEATY / SMOKY · CITRUS FRUIT
SHARP / ACIDIC · DRIED FRUIT
ASTRINGENT · HERBAL / VEGETAL
ROASTED / WOODY · SPICES
MOLASSES · SWEET / CANDIED

FLAVOR NOTES

SMELL / SCENT NOTES

OTHER NOTES

BOURBON LOG

BOURBON NAME		DATE TASTED

PRODUCER	DISTILLERY

TYPE / GRADE	COUNTRY OF ORIGIN

STILL TYPE	REGION

AGE	ALCOHOL %	PRICE	BOTTLE SIZE

QUALITY RATING

1	2	3	4	5	6	7	8	9	10

VALUE FOR MONEY

1	2	3	4	5	6	7	8	9	10

COLOR METER

- BLACK
- DARK BROWN
- MAHOGANY
- BRICK
- DARK AMBER
- AMBER
- GOLD
- STRAW
- CLEAR

FLAVOR WHEEL

BALANCE
HEAT / ABM _____ %
FINISH
FRESH FRUIT
BODY
PEATY / SMOKY
DARK FRUIT
SHARP / ACIDIC
CITRUS FRUIT
ASTRINGENT
DRIED FRUIT
ROASTED / WOODY
HERBAL / VEGETAL
MOLASSES
SPICES
SWEET / CANDIED

FLAVOR NOTES

SMELL / SCENT NOTES

OTHER NOTES

BOURBON NAME		DATE TASTED	

PRODUCER	DISTILLERY

TYPE / GRADE	COUNTRY OF ORIGIN

STILL TYPE	REGION

AGE	ALCOHOL %	PRICE	BOTTLE SIZE

QUALITY RATING

1	2	3	4	5	6	7	8	9	10

VALUE FOR MONEY

1	2	3	4	5	6	7	8	9	10

COLOR METER

BLACK

DARK BROWN

MAHOGANY

BRICK

DARK AMBER

AMBER

GOLD

STRAW

CLEAR

FLAVOR WHEEL

BALANCE
FINISH
BODY
PEATY / SMOKY
SHARP / ACIDIC
ASTRINGENT
ROASTED / WOODY
MOLASSES
SWEET / CANDIED
SPICES
HERBAL / VEGETAL
DRIED FRUIT
CITRUS FRUIT
DARK FRUIT
FRESH FRUIT
HEAT / ABM _____ %

FLAVOR NOTES

SMELL / SCENT NOTES

OTHER NOTES

BOURBON LOG

BOURBON NAME	DATE TASTED

PRODUCER	DISTILLERY

TYPE / GRADE	COUNTRY OF ORIGIN

STILL TYPE	REGION

AGE	ALCOHOL %	PRICE	BOTTLE SIZE

QUALITY RATING

1	2	3	4	5	6	7	8	9	10

VALUE FOR MONEY

1	2	3	4	5	6	7	8	9	10

COLOR METER

- BLACK
- DARK BROWN
- MAHOGANY
- BRICK
- DARK AMBER
- AMBER
- GOLD
- STRAW
- CLEAR

FLAVOR WHEEL

BALANCE
HEAT / ABM _____ %
FINISH
FRESH FRUIT
BODY
DARK FRUIT
PEATY / SMOKY
CITRUS FRUIT
SHARP / ACIDIC
DRIED FRUIT
ASTRINGENT
ROASTED / WOODY
HERBAL / VEGETAL
MOLASSES
SPICES
SWEET / CANDIED

FLAVOR NOTES

SMELL / SCENT NOTES

OTHER NOTES

BOURBON NAME	DATE TASTED

PRODUCER	DISTILLERY

TYPE / GRADE	COUNTRY OF ORIGIN

STILL TYPE	REGION

AGE	ALCOHOL %	PRICE	BOTTLE SIZE

QUALITY RATING

1	2	3	4	5	6	7	8	9	10

VALUE FOR MONEY

1	2	3	4	5	6	7	8	9	10

COLOR METER

- BLACK
- DARK BROWN
- MAHOGANY
- BRICK
- DARK AMBER
- AMBER
- GOLD
- STRAW
- CLEAR

FLAVOR WHEEL

BALANCE, FINISH, BODY, PEATY / SMOKY, SHARP / ACIDIC, ASTRINGENT, ROASTED / WOODY, MOLASSES, SWEET / CANDIED, SPICES, HERBAL / VEGETAL, DRIED FRUIT, CITRUS FRUIT, DARK FRUIT, FRESH FRUIT, HEAT / ABM _____ %

FLAVOR NOTES

SMELL / SCENT NOTES

OTHER NOTES

BOURBON LOG

BOURBON NAME	DATE TASTED

PRODUCER	DISTILLERY

TYPE / GRADE	COUNTRY OF ORIGIN

STILL TYPE	REGION

AGE	ALCOHOL %	PRICE	BOTTLE SIZE

QUALITY RATING

1	2	3	4	5	6	7	8	9	10

VALUE FOR MONEY

1	2	3	4	5	6	7	8	9	10

COLOR METER

- BLACK
- DARK BROWN
- MAHOGANY
- BRICK
- DARK AMBER
- AMBER
- GOLD
- STRAW
- CLEAR

FLAVOR WHEEL

HEAT / ABM _____ %

BALANCE
FINISH
BODY
PEATY / SMOKY
SHARP / ACIDIC
ASTRINGENT
ROASTED / WOODY
MOLASSES
SWEET / CANDIED
SPICES
HERBAL / VEGETAL
DRIED FRUIT
CITRUS FRUIT
DARK FRUIT
FRESH FRUIT

FLAVOR NOTES

SMELL / SCENT NOTES

OTHER NOTES

BOURBON NAME

DATE TASTED

PRODUCER

DISTILLERY

TYPE / GRADE

COUNTRY OF ORIGIN

STILL TYPE

REGION

AGE	ALCOHOL %	PRICE	BOTTLE SIZE

QUALITY RATING

1	2	3	4	5	6	7	8	9	10

VALUE FOR MONEY

1	2	3	4	5	6	7	8	9	10

COLOR METER

BLACK
DARK BROWN
MAHOGANY
BRICK
DARK AMBER
AMBER
GOLD
STRAW
CLEAR

FLAVOR WHEEL

BALANCE
FINISH
BODY
PEATY / SMOKY
SHARP / ACIDIC
ASTRINGENT
ROASTED / WOODY
MOLASSES
SWEET / CANDIED
SPICES
HERBAL / VEGETAL
DRIED FRUIT
CITRUS FRUIT
DARK FRUIT
FRESH FRUIT
HEAT / ABM _____ %

FLAVOR NOTES

SMELL / SCENT NOTES

OTHER NOTES

BOURBON LOG

BOURBON NAME		DATE TASTED

PRODUCER	DISTILLERY

TYPE / GRADE	COUNTRY OF ORIGIN

STILL TYPE	REGION

AGE	ALCOHOL %	PRICE	BOTTLE SIZE

QUALITY RATING

1	2	3	4	5	6	7	8	9	10

VALUE FOR MONEY

1	2	3	4	5	6	7	8	9	10

COLOR METER	FLAVOR WHEEL	FLAVOR NOTES

COLOR METER

- BLACK
- DARK BROWN
- MAHOGANY
- BRICK
- DARK AMBER
- AMBER
- GOLD
- STRAW
- CLEAR

FLAVOR WHEEL

HEAT / ABM _____ %

BALANCE
FINISH
BODY
PEATY / SMOKY
SHARP / ACIDIC
ASTRINGENT
ROASTED / WOODY
MOLASSES
SWEET / CANDIED
SPICES
HERBAL / VEGETAL
DRIED FRUIT
CITRUS FRUIT
DARK FRUIT
FRESH FRUIT

FLAVOR NOTES

SMELL / SCENT NOTES	OTHER NOTES

BOURBON NAME		DATE TASTED

PRODUCER	DISTILLERY

TYPE / GRADE	COUNTRY OF ORIGIN

STILL TYPE	REGION

AGE	ALCOHOL %	PRICE	BOTTLE SIZE

QUALITY RATING

1	2	3	4	5	6	7	8	9	10

VALUE FOR MONEY

1	2	3	4	5	6	7	8	9	10

COLOR METER

- BLACK
- DARK BROWN
- MAHOGANY
- BRICK
- DARK AMBER
- AMBER
- GOLD
- STRAW
- CLEAR

FLAVOR WHEEL

BALANCE
HEAT / ABM _____ %
FINISH
FRESH FRUIT
BODY
DARK FRUIT
PEATY / SMOKY
SHARP / ACIDIC
CITRUS FRUIT
DRIED FRUIT
ASTRINGENT
HERBAL / VEGETAL
ROASTED / WOODY
SPICES
MOLASSES
SWEET / CANDIED

FLAVOR NOTES

SMELL / SCENT NOTES	OTHER NOTES

BOURBON LOG

BOURBON NAME	DATE TASTED

PRODUCER	DISTILLERY

TYPE / GRADE	COUNTRY OF ORIGIN

STILL TYPE	REGION

AGE	ALCOHOL %	PRICE	BOTTLE SIZE

QUALITY RATING	VALUE FOR MONEY
1 2 3 4 5 6 7 8 9 10	1 2 3 4 5 6 7 8 9 10

COLOR METER

- BLACK
- DARK BROWN
- MAHOGANY
- BRICK
- DARK AMBER
- AMBER
- GOLD
- STRAW
- CLEAR

FLAVOR WHEEL

BALANCE · HEAT / ABM _____ %
FINISH
BODY
FRESH FRUIT
PEATY / SMOKY
DARK FRUIT
SHARP / ACIDIC
CITRUS FRUIT
ASTRINGENT
DRIED FRUIT
ROASTED / WOODY
HERBAL / VEGETAL
MOLASSES
SPICES
SWEET / CANDIED

FLAVOR NOTES

SMELL / SCENT NOTES	OTHER NOTES

BOURBON NAME		DATE TASTED

PRODUCER	DISTILLERY

TYPE / GRADE	COUNTRY OF ORIGIN

STILL TYPE	REGION

AGE	ALCOHOL %	PRICE	BOTTLE SIZE

QUALITY RATING

1	2	3	4	5	6	7	8	9	10

VALUE FOR MONEY

1	2	3	4	5	6	7	8	9	10

COLOR METER

- BLACK
- DARK BROWN
- MAHOGANY
- BRICK
- DARK AMBER
- AMBER
- GOLD
- STRAW
- CLEAR

FLAVOR WHEEL

HEAT / ABM _____ %

BALANCE
FINISH
BODY
PEATY / SMOKY
SHARP / ACIDIC
ASTRINGENT
ROASTED / WOODY
MOLASSES
SWEET / CANDIED
SPICES
HERBAL / VEGETAL
DRIED FRUIT
CITRUS FRUIT
DARK FRUIT
FRESH FRUIT

FLAVOR NOTES

SMELL / SCENT NOTES

OTHER NOTES

BOURBON LOG

BOURBON NAME		DATE TASTED

PRODUCER	DISTILLERY

TYPE / GRADE	COUNTRY OF ORIGIN

STILL TYPE	REGION

AGE	ALCOHOL %	PRICE	BOTTLE SIZE

QUALITY RATING

1	2	3	4	5	6	7	8	9	10

VALUE FOR MONEY

1	2	3	4	5	6	7	8	9	10

COLOR METER

- BLACK
- DARK BROWN
- MAHOGANY
- BRICK
- DARK AMBER
- AMBER
- GOLD
- STRAW
- CLEAR

FLAVOR WHEEL

BALANCE
HEAT / ABM _____ %
FINISH
FRESH FRUIT
BODY
PEATY / SMOKY
DARK FRUIT
SHARP / ACIDIC
CITRUS FRUIT
ASTRINGENT
DRIED FRUIT
ROASTED / WOODY
HERBAL / VEGETAL
MOLASSES
SPICES
SWEET / CANDIED

FLAVOR NOTES

SMELL / SCENT NOTES

OTHER NOTES

BOURBON NAME	DATE TASTED

PRODUCER	DISTILLERY

TYPE / GRADE	COUNTRY OF ORIGIN

STILL TYPE	REGION

AGE	ALCOHOL %	PRICE	BOTTLE SIZE

QUALITY RATING

1	2	3	4	5	6	7	8	9	10

VALUE FOR MONEY

1	2	3	4	5	6	7	8	9	10

COLOR METER

- BLACK
- DARK BROWN
- MAHOGANY
- BRICK
- DARK AMBER
- AMBER
- GOLD
- STRAW
- CLEAR

FLAVOR WHEEL

HEAT / ABM _____ %

BALANCE
FINISH
BODY
PEATY / SMOKY
SHARP / ACIDIC
ASTRINGENT
ROASTED / WOODY
MOLASSES
SWEET / CANDIED
SPICES
HERBAL / VEGETAL
DRIED FRUIT
CITRUS FRUIT
DARK FRUIT
FRESH FRUIT

FLAVOR NOTES

SMELL / SCENT NOTES

OTHER NOTES

BOURBON NAME		DATE TASTED

PRODUCER	DISTILLERY

TYPE / GRADE	COUNTRY OF ORIGIN

STILL TYPE	REGION

AGE	ALCOHOL %	PRICE	BOTTLE SIZE

QUALITY RATING

1	2	3	4	5	6	7	8	9	10

VALUE FOR MONEY

1	2	3	4	5	6	7	8	9	10

COLOR METER

BLACK
DARK BROWN
MAHOGANY
BRICK
DARK AMBER
AMBER
GOLD
STRAW
CLEAR

FLAVOR WHEEL

HEAT / ABM _____ %

BALANCE
FINISH
BODY
PEATY / SMOKY
SHARP / ACIDIC
ASTRINGENT
ROASTED / WOODY
MOLASSES
SWEET / CANDIED
SPICES
HERBAL / VEGETAL
DRIED FRUIT
CITRUS FRUIT
DARK FRUIT
FRESH FRUIT

FLAVOR NOTES

SMELL / SCENT NOTES	OTHER NOTES

BOURBON NAME		DATE TASTED

PRODUCER	DISTILLERY

TYPE / GRADE	COUNTRY OF ORIGIN

STILL TYPE	REGION

AGE	ALCOHOL %	PRICE	BOTTLE SIZE

QUALITY RATING

1	2	3	4	5	6	7	8	9	10

VALUE FOR MONEY

1	2	3	4	5	6	7	8	9	10

COLOR METER

BLACK
DARK BROWN
MAHOGANY
BRICK
DARK AMBER
AMBER
GOLD
STRAW
CLEAR

FLAVOR WHEEL

BALANCE, HEAT / ABM _____ %, FINISH, FRESH FRUIT, BODY, DARK FRUIT, PEATY / SMOKY, CITRUS FRUIT, SHARP / ACIDIC, DRIED FRUIT, ASTRINGENT, HERBAL / VEGETAL, ROASTED / WOODY, SPICES, MOLASSES, SWEET / CANDIED

FLAVOR NOTES

SMELL / SCENT NOTES

OTHER NOTES

BOURBON LOG

BOURBON NAME		DATE TASTED

PRODUCER	DISTILLERY

TYPE / GRADE	COUNTRY OF ORIGIN

STILL TYPE	REGION

AGE	ALCOHOL %	PRICE	BOTTLE SIZE

QUALITY RATING

1	2	3	4	5	6	7	8	9	10

VALUE FOR MONEY

1	2	3	4	5	6	7	8	9	10

COLOR METER

- BLACK
- DARK BROWN
- MAHOGANY
- BRICK
- DARK AMBER
- AMBER
- GOLD
- STRAW
- CLEAR

FLAVOR WHEEL

BALANCE
HEAT / ABM _____ %
FINISH
FRESH FRUIT
BODY
DARK FRUIT
PEATY / SMOKY
CITRUS FRUIT
SHARP / ACIDIC
DRIED FRUIT
ASTRINGENT
ROASTED / WOODY
HERBAL / VEGETAL
MOLASSES
SPICES
SWEET / CANDIED

FLAVOR NOTES

SMELL / SCENT NOTES

OTHER NOTES

BOURBON NAME		DATE TASTED

PRODUCER	DISTILLERY

TYPE / GRADE	COUNTRY OF ORIGIN

STILL TYPE	REGION

AGE	ALCOHOL %	PRICE	BOTTLE SIZE

QUALITY RATING

1	2	3	4	5	6	7	8	9	10

VALUE FOR MONEY

1	2	3	4	5	6	7	8	9	10

COLOR METER

- BLACK
- DARK BROWN
- MAHOGANY
- BRICK
- DARK AMBER
- AMBER
- GOLD
- STRAW
- CLEAR

FLAVOR WHEEL

HEAT / ABM _____ %

BALANCE, FINISH, BODY, PEATY / SMOKY, SHARP / ACIDIC, ASTRINGENT, ROASTED / WOODY, MOLASSES, SWEET / CANDIED, SPICES, HERBAL / VEGETAL, DRIED FRUIT, CITRUS FRUIT, DARK FRUIT, FRESH FRUIT

FLAVOR NOTES

SMELL / SCENT NOTES

OTHER NOTES

BOURBON LOG

BOURBON NAME	DATE TASTED

PRODUCER	DISTILLERY

TYPE / GRADE	COUNTRY OF ORIGIN

STILL TYPE	REGION

AGE	ALCOHOL %	PRICE	BOTTLE SIZE

QUALITY RATING

1	2	3	4	5	6	7	8	9	10

VALUE FOR MONEY

1	2	3	4	5	6	7	8	9	10

COLOR METER

- BLACK
- DARK BROWN
- MAHOGANY
- BRICK
- DARK AMBER
- AMBER
- GOLD
- STRAW
- CLEAR

FLAVOR WHEEL

BALANCE
HEAT / ABM _____ %
FINISH
FRESH FRUIT
BODY
DARK FRUIT
PEATY / SMOKY
CITRUS FRUIT
SHARP / ACIDIC
DRIED FRUIT
ASTRINGENT
ROASTED / WOODY
HERBAL / VEGETAL
MOLASSES
SPICES
SWEET / CANDIED

FLAVOR NOTES

SMELL / SCENT NOTES

OTHER NOTES

BOURBON NAME		DATE TASTED

PRODUCER	DISTILLERY

TYPE / GRADE	COUNTRY OF ORIGIN

STILL TYPE	REGION

AGE	ALCOHOL %	PRICE	BOTTLE SIZE

QUALITY RATING

1	2	3	4	5	6	7	8	9	10

VALUE FOR MONEY

1	2	3	4	5	6	7	8	9	10

COLOR METER

BLACK
DARK BROWN
MAHOGANY
BRICK
DARK AMBER
AMBER
GOLD
STRAW
CLEAR

FLAVOR WHEEL

HEAT / ABM ____ %

BALANCE, FINISH, BODY, PEATY / SMOKY, SHARP / ACIDIC, ASTRINGENT, ROASTED / WOODY, MOLASSES, SWEET / CANDIED, SPICES, HERBAL / VEGETAL, DRIED FRUIT, CITRUS FRUIT, DARK FRUIT, FRESH FRUIT

FLAVOR NOTES

SMELL / SCENT NOTES

OTHER NOTES

BOURBON LOG

BOURBON NAME		DATE TASTED

PRODUCER	DISTILLERY

TYPE / GRADE	COUNTRY OF ORIGIN

STILL TYPE	REGION

AGE	ALCOHOL %	PRICE	BOTTLE SIZE

QUALITY RATING

1	2	3	4	5	6	7	8	9	10

VALUE FOR MONEY

1	2	3	4	5	6	7	8	9	10

COLOR METER

- BLACK
- DARK BROWN
- MAHOGANY
- BRICK
- DARK AMBER
- AMBER
- GOLD
- STRAW
- CLEAR

FLAVOR WHEEL

BALANCE HEAT / ABM _____ %
FINISH
BODY
FRESH FRUIT
PEATY / SMOKY
DARK FRUIT
SHARP / ACIDIC
CITRUS FRUIT
ASTRINGENT
DRIED FRUIT
ROASTED / WOODY
HERBAL / VEGETAL
MOLASSES
SPICES
SWEET / CANDIED

FLAVOR NOTES

SMELL / SCENT NOTES

OTHER NOTES

BOURBON NAME	DATE TASTED

PRODUCER	DISTILLERY

TYPE / GRADE	COUNTRY OF ORIGIN

STILL TYPE	REGION

AGE	ALCOHOL %	PRICE	BOTTLE SIZE

QUALITY RATING

1	2	3	4	5	6	7	8	9	10

VALUE FOR MONEY

1	2	3	4	5	6	7	8	9	10

COLOR METER

- BLACK
- DARK BROWN
- MAHOGANY
- BRICK
- DARK AMBER
- AMBER
- GOLD
- STRAW
- CLEAR

FLAVOR WHEEL

BALANCE · HEAT / ABM _____ %
FINISH · FRESH FRUIT
BODY · DARK FRUIT
PEATY / SMOKY · CITRUS FRUIT
SHARP / ACIDIC · DRIED FRUIT
ASTRINGENT · HERBAL / VEGETAL
ROASTED / WOODY · SPICES
MOLASSES · SWEET / CANDIED

FLAVOR NOTES

SMELL / SCENT NOTES

OTHER NOTES

BOURBON LOG

BOURBON NAME		DATE TASTED

PRODUCER	DISTILLERY

TYPE / GRADE	COUNTRY OF ORIGIN

STILL TYPE	REGION

AGE	ALCOHOL %	PRICE	BOTTLE SIZE

QUALITY RATING

1	2	3	4	5	6	7	8	9	10

VALUE FOR MONEY

1	2	3	4	5	6	7	8	9	10

COLOR METER

- BLACK
- DARK BROWN
- MAHOGANY
- BRICK
- DARK AMBER
- AMBER
- GOLD
- STRAW
- CLEAR

FLAVOR WHEEL

BALANCE
HEAT / ABM _____ %
FINISH
BODY
FRESH FRUIT
PEATY / SMOKY
DARK FRUIT
SHARP / ACIDIC
CITRUS FRUIT
ASTRINGENT
DRIED FRUIT
ROASTED / WOODY
HERBAL / VEGETAL
MOLASSES
SPICES
SWEET / CANDIED

FLAVOR NOTES

SMELL / SCENT NOTES

OTHER NOTES

BOURBON NAME		DATE TASTED

PRODUCER	DISTILLERY

TYPE / GRADE	COUNTRY OF ORIGIN

STILL TYPE	REGION

AGE	ALCOHOL %	PRICE	BOTTLE SIZE

QUALITY RATING

1	2	3	4	5	6	7	8	9	10

VALUE FOR MONEY

1	2	3	4	5	6	7	8	9	10

COLOR METER

- BLACK
- DARK BROWN
- MAHOGANY
- BRICK
- DARK AMBER
- AMBER
- GOLD
- STRAW
- CLEAR

FLAVOR WHEEL

BALANCE · HEAT / ABM _____ %
FINISH
BODY · FRESH FRUIT
PEATY / SMOKY · DARK FRUIT
SHARP / ACIDIC · CITRUS FRUIT
ASTRINGENT · DRIED FRUIT
ROASTED / WOODY · HERBAL / VEGETAL
MOLASSES · SPICES
SWEET / CANDIED

FLAVOR NOTES

SMELL / SCENT NOTES

OTHER NOTES

BOURBON NAME		DATE TASTED

PRODUCER	DISTILLERY

TYPE / GRADE	COUNTRY OF ORIGIN

STILL TYPE	REGION

AGE	ALCOHOL %	PRICE	BOTTLE SIZE

QUALITY RATING

1	2	3	4	5	6	7	8	9	10

VALUE FOR MONEY

1	2	3	4	5	6	7	8	9	10

COLOR METER	FLAVOR WHEEL	FLAVOR NOTES

COLOR METER

- BLACK
- DARK BROWN
- MAHOGANY
- BRICK
- DARK AMBER
- AMBER
- GOLD
- STRAW
- CLEAR

FLAVOR WHEEL

HEAT / ABM _____ %

BALANCE
FINISH
BODY
PEATY / SMOKY
SHARP / ACIDIC
ASTRINGENT
ROASTED / WOODY
MOLASSES
SWEET / CANDIED
SPICES
HERBAL / VEGETAL
DRIED FRUIT
CITRUS FRUIT
DARK FRUIT
FRESH FRUIT

FLAVOR NOTES

SMELL / SCENT NOTES	OTHER NOTES

BOURBON NAME		DATE TASTED

PRODUCER	DISTILLERY

TYPE / GRADE	COUNTRY OF ORIGIN

STILL TYPE	REGION

AGE	ALCOHOL %	PRICE	BOTTLE SIZE

QUALITY RATING

1	2	3	4	5	6	7	8	9	10

VALUE FOR MONEY

1	2	3	4	5	6	7	8	9	10

COLOR METER

- BLACK
- DARK BROWN
- MAHOGANY
- BRICK
- DARK AMBER
- AMBER
- GOLD
- STRAW
- CLEAR

FLAVOR WHEEL

HEAT / ABM _____ %

BALANCE
FINISH
BODY
PEATY / SMOKY
SHARP / ACIDIC
ASTRINGENT
ROASTED / WOODY
MOLASSES
SWEET / CANDIED
SPICES
HERBAL / VEGETAL
DRIED FRUIT
CITRUS FRUIT
DARK FRUIT
FRESH FRUIT

FLAVOR NOTES

SMELL / SCENT NOTES

OTHER NOTES

BOURBON LOG

BOURBON NAME	DATE TASTED

PRODUCER	DISTILLERY

TYPE / GRADE	COUNTRY OF ORIGIN

STILL TYPE	REGION

AGE	ALCOHOL %	PRICE	BOTTLE SIZE

QUALITY RATING

1	2	3	4	5	6	7	8	9	10

VALUE FOR MONEY

1	2	3	4	5	6	7	8	9	10

COLOR METER	FLAVOR WHEEL	FLAVOR NOTES

COLOR METER

- BLACK
- DARK BROWN
- MAHOGANY
- BRICK
- DARK AMBER
- AMBER
- GOLD
- STRAW
- CLEAR

FLAVOR WHEEL

BALANCE — HEAT / ABM _____ %
FINISH
BODY — FRESH FRUIT
PEATY / SMOKY — DARK FRUIT
SHARP / ACIDIC — CITRUS FRUIT
ASTRINGENT — DRIED FRUIT
ROASTED / WOODY — HERBAL / VEGETAL
MOLASSES — SPICES
SWEET / CANDIED

SMELL / SCENT NOTES	OTHER NOTES

BOURBON NAME		DATE TASTED	

PRODUCER	DISTILLERY

TYPE / GRADE	COUNTRY OF ORIGIN

STILL TYPE	REGION

AGE	ALCOHOL %	PRICE	BOTTLE SIZE

QUALITY RATING

1	2	3	4	5	6	7	8	9	10

VALUE FOR MONEY

1	2	3	4	5	6	7	8	9	10

COLOR METER

BLACK

DARK BROWN

MAHOGANY

BRICK

DARK AMBER

AMBER

GOLD

STRAW

CLEAR

FLAVOR WHEEL

BALANCE
FINISH
BODY
PEATY / SMOKY
SHARP / ACIDIC
ASTRINGENT
ROASTED / WOODY
MOLASSES
SWEET / CANDIED
SPICES
HERBAL / VEGETAL
DRIED FRUIT
CITRUS FRUIT
DARK FRUIT
FRESH FRUIT
HEAT / ABM _____ %

FLAVOR NOTES

SMELL / SCENT NOTES

OTHER NOTES

BOURBON LOG

BOURBON NAME		DATE TASTED

PRODUCER	DISTILLERY

TYPE / GRADE	COUNTRY OF ORIGIN

STILL TYPE	REGION

AGE	ALCOHOL %	PRICE	BOTTLE SIZE

QUALITY RATING

1	2	3	4	5	6	7	8	9	10

VALUE FOR MONEY

1	2	3	4	5	6	7	8	9	10

COLOR METER

- BLACK
- DARK BROWN
- MAHOGANY
- BRICK
- DARK AMBER
- AMBER
- GOLD
- STRAW
- CLEAR

FLAVOR WHEEL

BALANCE — HEAT / ABM _____ %
FINISH — FRESH FRUIT
BODY — DARK FRUIT
PEATY / SMOKY — CITRUS FRUIT
SHARP / ACIDIC — DRIED FRUIT
ASTRINGENT — HERBAL / VEGETAL
ROASTED / WOODY — SPICES
MOLASSES — SWEET / CANDIED

FLAVOR NOTES

SMELL / SCENT NOTES

OTHER NOTES

48

BOURBON NAME		DATE TASTED

PRODUCER	DISTILLERY

TYPE / GRADE	COUNTRY OF ORIGIN

STILL TYPE	REGION

AGE	ALCOHOL %	PRICE	BOTTLE SIZE

QUALITY RATING

1	2	3	4	5	6	7	8	9	10

VALUE FOR MONEY

1	2	3	4	5	6	7	8	9	10

COLOR METER

- BLACK
- DARK BROWN
- MAHOGANY
- BRICK
- DARK AMBER
- AMBER
- GOLD
- STRAW
- CLEAR

FLAVOR WHEEL

BALANCE · HEAT / ABM _____ % · FINISH · FRESH FRUIT · BODY · DARK FRUIT · PEATY / SMOKY · CITRUS FRUIT · SHARP / ACIDIC · DRIED FRUIT · ASTRINGENT · HERBAL / VEGETAL · ROASTED / WOODY · SPICES · MOLASSES · SWEET / CANDIED

FLAVOR NOTES

SMELL / SCENT NOTES	OTHER NOTES

BOURBON LOG

BOURBON NAME	DATE TASTED

PRODUCER	DISTILLERY

TYPE / GRADE	COUNTRY OF ORIGIN

STILL TYPE	REGION

AGE	ALCOHOL %	PRICE	BOTTLE SIZE

QUALITY RATING

1	2	3	4	5	6	7	8	9	10

VALUE FOR MONEY

1	2	3	4	5	6	7	8	9	10

COLOR METER

- BLACK
- DARK BROWN
- MAHOGANY
- BRICK
- DARK AMBER
- AMBER
- GOLD
- STRAW
- CLEAR

FLAVOR WHEEL

BALANCE • HEAT / ABM _____ %
FINISH
BODY
FRESH FRUIT
PEATY / SMOKY
DARK FRUIT
SHARP / ACIDIC
CITRUS FRUIT
ASTRINGENT
DRIED FRUIT
ROASTED / WOODY
HERBAL / VEGETAL
MOLASSES
SPICES
SWEET / CANDIED

FLAVOR NOTES

SMELL / SCENT NOTES

OTHER NOTES

BOURBON NAME		DATE TASTED

PRODUCER	DISTILLERY

TYPE / GRADE	COUNTRY OF ORIGIN

STILL TYPE	REGION

AGE	ALCOHOL %	PRICE	BOTTLE SIZE

QUALITY RATING

1	2	3	4	5	6	7	8	9	10

VALUE FOR MONEY

1	2	3	4	5	6	7	8	9	10

COLOR METER

- BLACK
- DARK BROWN
- MAHOGANY
- BRICK
- DARK AMBER
- AMBER
- GOLD
- STRAW
- CLEAR

FLAVOR WHEEL

HEAT / ABM _____ %

BALANCE
FINISH
BODY
PEATY / SMOKY
SHARP / ACIDIC
ASTRINGENT
ROASTED / WOODY
MOLASSES
SWEET / CANDIED
SPICES
HERBAL / VEGETAL
DRIED FRUIT
CITRUS FRUIT
DARK FRUIT
FRESH FRUIT

FLAVOR NOTES

SMELL / SCENT NOTES

OTHER NOTES

BOURBON LOG

BOURBON NAME		DATE TASTED

PRODUCER	DISTILLERY

TYPE / GRADE	COUNTRY OF ORIGIN

STILL TYPE	REGION

AGE	ALCOHOL %	PRICE	BOTTLE SIZE

QUALITY RATING

1	2	3	4	5	6	7	8	9	10

VALUE FOR MONEY

1	2	3	4	5	6	7	8	9	10

COLOR METER	FLAVOR WHEEL	FLAVOR NOTES

COLOR METER

- BLACK
- DARK BROWN
- MAHOGANY
- BRICK
- DARK AMBER
- AMBER
- GOLD
- STRAW
- CLEAR

FLAVOR WHEEL

BALANCE — HEAT / ABM _____ %
FINISH
FRESH FRUIT
BODY
PEATY / SMOKY
DARK FRUIT
SHARP / ACIDIC
CITRUS FRUIT
ASTRINGENT
DRIED FRUIT
ROASTED / WOODY
HERBAL / VEGETAL
MOLASSES
SPICES
SWEET / CANDIED

SMELL / SCENT NOTES	OTHER NOTES

BOURBON NAME		DATE TASTED

PRODUCER	DISTILLERY

TYPE / GRADE	COUNTRY OF ORIGIN

STILL TYPE	REGION

AGE	ALCOHOL %	PRICE	BOTTLE SIZE

QUALITY RATING

1	2	3	4	5	6	7	8	9	10

VALUE FOR MONEY

1	2	3	4	5	6	7	8	9	10

COLOR METER

- BLACK
- DARK BROWN
- MAHOGANY
- BRICK
- DARK AMBER
- AMBER
- GOLD
- STRAW
- CLEAR

FLAVOR WHEEL

BALANCE — HEAT / ABM _____ %
FINISH
BODY
FRESH FRUIT
PEATY / SMOKY
DARK FRUIT
SHARP / ACIDIC
CITRUS FRUIT
ASTRINGENT
DRIED FRUIT
ROASTED / WOODY
HERBAL / VEGETAL
MOLASSES
SPICES
SWEET / CANDIED

FLAVOR NOTES

SMELL / SCENT NOTES

OTHER NOTES

BOURBON LOG

BOURBON NAME	DATE TASTED

PRODUCER	DISTILLERY

TYPE / GRADE	COUNTRY OF ORIGIN

STILL TYPE	REGION

AGE	ALCOHOL %	PRICE	BOTTLE SIZE

QUALITY RATING

1	2	3	4	5	6	7	8	9	10

VALUE FOR MONEY

1	2	3	4	5	6	7	8	9	10

COLOR METER

- BLACK
- DARK BROWN
- MAHOGANY
- BRICK
- DARK AMBER
- AMBER
- GOLD
- STRAW
- CLEAR

FLAVOR WHEEL

HEAT / ABM _____ %

BALANCE, FINISH, BODY, PEATY / SMOKY, SHARP / ACIDIC, ASTRINGENT, ROASTED / WOODY, MOLASSES, SWEET / CANDIED, SPICES, HERBAL / VEGETAL, DRIED FRUIT, CITRUS FRUIT, DARK FRUIT, FRESH FRUIT

FLAVOR NOTES

SMELL / SCENT NOTES	OTHER NOTES

BOURBON NAME		DATE TASTED

PRODUCER	DISTILLERY

TYPE / GRADE	COUNTRY OF ORIGIN

STILL TYPE	REGION

AGE	ALCOHOL %	PRICE	BOTTLE SIZE

QUALITY RATING

1	2	3	4	5	6	7	8	9	10

VALUE FOR MONEY

1	2	3	4	5	6	7	8	9	10

COLOR METER

- BLACK
- DARK BROWN
- MAHOGANY
- BRICK
- DARK AMBER
- AMBER
- GOLD
- STRAW
- CLEAR

FLAVOR WHEEL

BALANCE
HEAT / ABM _____ %
FINISH
FRESH FRUIT
BODY
PEATY / SMOKY
DARK FRUIT
SHARP / ACIDIC
CITRUS FRUIT
ASTRINGENT
DRIED FRUIT
ROASTED / WOODY
HERBAL / VEGETAL
MOLASSES
SPICES
SWEET / CANDIED

FLAVOR NOTES

SMELL / SCENT NOTES

OTHER NOTES

BOURBON LOG

BOURBON NAME	DATE TASTED

PRODUCER	DISTILLERY

TYPE / GRADE	COUNTRY OF ORIGIN

STILL TYPE	REGION

AGE	ALCOHOL %	PRICE	BOTTLE SIZE

QUALITY RATING

1	2	3	4	5	6	7	8	9	10

VALUE FOR MONEY

1	2	3	4	5	6	7	8	9	10

COLOR METER

- BLACK
- DARK BROWN
- MAHOGANY
- BRICK
- DARK AMBER
- AMBER
- GOLD
- STRAW
- CLEAR

FLAVOR WHEEL

BALANCE
FINISH
BODY
PEATY / SMOKY
SHARP / ACIDIC
ASTRINGENT
ROASTED / WOODY
MOLASSES
SWEET / CANDIED
SPICES
HERBAL / VEGETAL
DRIED FRUIT
CITRUS FRUIT
DARK FRUIT
FRESH FRUIT
HEAT / ABM _____ %

FLAVOR NOTES

SMELL / SCENT NOTES

OTHER NOTES

BOURBON NAME		DATE TASTED

PRODUCER	DISTILLERY

TYPE / GRADE	COUNTRY OF ORIGIN

STILL TYPE	REGION

AGE	ALCOHOL %	PRICE	BOTTLE SIZE

QUALITY RATING

1	2	3	4	5	6	7	8	9	10

VALUE FOR MONEY

1	2	3	4	5	6	7	8	9	10

COLOR METER

- BLACK
- DARK BROWN
- MAHOGANY
- BRICK
- DARK AMBER
- AMBER
- GOLD
- STRAW
- CLEAR

FLAVOR WHEEL

BALANCE
FINISH
BODY
PEATY / SMOKY
SHARP / ACIDIC
ASTRINGENT
ROASTED / WOODY
MOLASSES
SWEET / CANDIED
SPICES
HERBAL / VEGETAL
DRIED FRUIT
CITRUS FRUIT
DARK FRUIT
FRESH FRUIT
HEAT / ABM _____ %

FLAVOR NOTES

SMELL / SCENT NOTES

OTHER NOTES

BOURBON LOG

BOURBON NAME	DATE TASTED

PRODUCER	DISTILLERY

TYPE / GRADE	COUNTRY OF ORIGIN

STILL TYPE	REGION

AGE	ALCOHOL %	PRICE	BOTTLE SIZE

QUALITY RATING

1	2	3	4	5	6	7	8	9	10

VALUE FOR MONEY

1	2	3	4	5	6	7	8	9	10

COLOR METER	FLAVOR WHEEL	FLAVOR NOTES

COLOR METER

- BLACK
- DARK BROWN
- MAHOGANY
- BRICK
- DARK AMBER
- AMBER
- GOLD
- STRAW
- CLEAR

FLAVOR WHEEL

BALANCE — HEAT / ABM _____ %
FINISH
BODY
FRESH FRUIT
PEATY / SMOKY
DARK FRUIT
SHARP / ACIDIC
CITRUS FRUIT
ASTRINGENT
DRIED FRUIT
ROASTED / WOODY
HERBAL / VEGETAL
MOLASSES
SPICES
SWEET / CANDIED

SMELL / SCENT NOTES	OTHER NOTES

BOURBON NAME		DATE TASTED

PRODUCER	DISTILLERY

TYPE / GRADE	COUNTRY OF ORIGIN

STILL TYPE	REGION

AGE	ALCOHOL %	PRICE	BOTTLE SIZE

QUALITY RATING

1	2	3	4	5	6	7	8	9	10

VALUE FOR MONEY

1	2	3	4	5	6	7	8	9	10

COLOR METER

- BLACK
- DARK BROWN
- MAHOGANY
- BRICK
- DARK AMBER
- AMBER
- GOLD
- STRAW
- CLEAR

FLAVOR WHEEL

BALANCE — HEAT / ABM _____ %

FINISH, FRESH FRUIT, BODY, PEATY / SMOKY, DARK FRUIT, SHARP / ACIDIC, CITRUS FRUIT, ASTRINGENT, DRIED FRUIT, ROASTED / WOODY, HERBAL / VEGETAL, MOLASSES, SPICES, SWEET / CANDIED

FLAVOR NOTES

SMELL / SCENT NOTES

OTHER NOTES

BOURBON LOG

BOURBON NAME		DATE TASTED

PRODUCER	DISTILLERY

TYPE / GRADE	COUNTRY OF ORIGIN

STILL TYPE	REGION

AGE	ALCOHOL %	PRICE	BOTTLE SIZE

QUALITY RATING

1	2	3	4	5	6	7	8	9	10

VALUE FOR MONEY

1	2	3	4	5	6	7	8	9	10

COLOR METER

- BLACK
- DARK BROWN
- MAHOGANY
- BRICK
- DARK AMBER
- AMBER
- GOLD
- STRAW
- CLEAR

FLAVOR WHEEL

BALANCE
HEAT / ABM _____ %
FINISH
FRESH FRUIT
BODY
PEATY / SMOKY
DARK FRUIT
SHARP / ACIDIC
CITRUS FRUIT
ASTRINGENT
DRIED FRUIT
ROASTED / WOODY
HERBAL / VEGETAL
MOLASSES
SPICES
SWEET / CANDIED

FLAVOR NOTES

SMELL / SCENT NOTES

OTHER NOTES

BOURBON NAME		DATE TASTED

PRODUCER	DISTILLERY

TYPE / GRADE	COUNTRY OF ORIGIN

STILL TYPE	REGION

AGE	ALCOHOL %	PRICE	BOTTLE SIZE

QUALITY RATING

1	2	3	4	5	6	7	8	9	10

VALUE FOR MONEY

1	2	3	4	5	6	7	8	9	10

COLOR METER

BLACK

DARK BROWN

MAHOGANY

BRICK

DARK AMBER

AMBER

GOLD

STRAW

CLEAR

FLAVOR WHEEL

BALANCE
FINISH
BODY
PEATY / SMOKY
SHARP / ACIDIC
ASTRINGENT
ROASTED / WOODY
MOLASSES
SWEET / CANDIED
SPICES
HERBAL / VEGETAL
DRIED FRUIT
CITRUS FRUIT
DARK FRUIT
FRESH FRUIT
HEAT / ABM _____ %

FLAVOR NOTES

SMELL / SCENT NOTES	OTHER NOTES

BOURBON LOG

BOURBON NAME	DATE TASTED

PRODUCER	DISTILLERY

TYPE / GRADE	COUNTRY OF ORIGIN

STILL TYPE	REGION

AGE	ALCOHOL %	PRICE	BOTTLE SIZE

QUALITY RATING

1	2	3	4	5	6	7	8	9	10

VALUE FOR MONEY

1	2	3	4	5	6	7	8	9	10

COLOR METER

- BLACK
- DARK BROWN
- MAHOGANY
- BRICK
- DARK AMBER
- AMBER
- GOLD
- STRAW
- CLEAR

FLAVOR WHEEL

HEAT / ABM _____ %

BALANCE, FINISH, BODY, PEATY / SMOKY, SHARP / ACIDIC, ASTRINGENT, ROASTED / WOODY, MOLASSES, SWEET / CANDIED, SPICES, HERBAL / VEGETAL, DRIED FRUIT, CITRUS FRUIT, DARK FRUIT, FRESH FRUIT

FLAVOR NOTES

SMELL / SCENT NOTES

OTHER NOTES

62

BOURBON NAME	DATE TASTED

PRODUCER	DISTILLERY

TYPE / GRADE	COUNTRY OF ORIGIN

STILL TYPE	REGION

AGE	ALCOHOL %	PRICE	BOTTLE SIZE

QUALITY RATING

1	2	3	4	5	6	7	8	9	10

VALUE FOR MONEY

1	2	3	4	5	6	7	8	9	10

COLOR METER

- BLACK
- DARK BROWN
- MAHOGANY
- BRICK
- DARK AMBER
- AMBER
- GOLD
- STRAW
- CLEAR

FLAVOR WHEEL

BALANCE
FINISH
BODY
PEATY / SMOKY
SHARP / ACIDIC
ASTRINGENT
ROASTED / WOODY
MOLASSES
SWEET / CANDIED
SPICES
HERBAL / VEGETAL
DRIED FRUIT
CITRUS FRUIT
DARK FRUIT
FRESH FRUIT
HEAT / ABM _____ %

FLAVOR NOTES

SMELL / SCENT NOTES	OTHER NOTES

BOURBON LOG

BOURBON NAME		DATE TASTED

PRODUCER	DISTILLERY

TYPE / GRADE	COUNTRY OF ORIGIN

STILL TYPE	REGION

AGE	ALCOHOL %	PRICE	BOTTLE SIZE

QUALITY RATING

1	2	3	4	5	6	7	8	9	10

VALUE FOR MONEY

1	2	3	4	5	6	7	8	9	10

COLOR METER

- BLACK
- DARK BROWN
- MAHOGANY
- BRICK
- DARK AMBER
- AMBER
- GOLD
- STRAW
- CLEAR

FLAVOR WHEEL

HEAT / ABM _____ %

BALANCE
FINISH
BODY
PEATY / SMOKY
SHARP / ACIDIC
ASTRINGENT
ROASTED / WOODY
MOLASSES
SWEET / CANDIED
SPICES
HERBAL / VEGETAL
DRIED FRUIT
CITRUS FRUIT
DARK FRUIT
FRESH FRUIT

FLAVOR NOTES

SMELL / SCENT NOTES

OTHER NOTES

64

BOURBON NAME		DATE TASTED

PRODUCER	DISTILLERY

TYPE / GRADE	COUNTRY OF ORIGIN

STILL TYPE	REGION

AGE	ALCOHOL %	PRICE	BOTTLE SIZE

QUALITY RATING

1	2	3	4	5	6	7	8	9	10

VALUE FOR MONEY

1	2	3	4	5	6	7	8	9	10

COLOR METER

- BLACK
- DARK BROWN
- MAHOGANY
- BRICK
- DARK AMBER
- AMBER
- GOLD
- STRAW
- CLEAR

FLAVOR WHEEL

BALANCE, HEAT / ABM ____ %, FINISH, FRESH FRUIT, BODY, DARK FRUIT, PEATY / SMOKY, CITRUS FRUIT, SHARP / ACIDIC, DRIED FRUIT, ASTRINGENT, HERBAL / VEGETAL, ROASTED / WOODY, SPICES, MOLASSES, SWEET / CANDIED

FLAVOR NOTES

SMELL / SCENT NOTES

OTHER NOTES

BOURBON LOG

BOURBON NAME	DATE TASTED

PRODUCER	DISTILLERY

TYPE / GRADE	COUNTRY OF ORIGIN

STILL TYPE	REGION

AGE	ALCOHOL %	PRICE	BOTTLE SIZE

QUALITY RATING

1	2	3	4	5	6	7	8	9	10

VALUE FOR MONEY

1	2	3	4	5	6	7	8	9	10

COLOR METER

- BLACK
- DARK BROWN
- MAHOGANY
- BRICK
- DARK AMBER
- AMBER
- GOLD
- STRAW
- CLEAR

FLAVOR WHEEL

HEAT / ABM _____ %

BALANCE
FINISH
BODY
PEATY / SMOKY
SHARP / ACIDIC
ASTRINGENT
ROASTED / WOODY
MOLASSES
SWEET / CANDIED
SPICES
HERBAL / VEGETAL
DRIED FRUIT
CITRUS FRUIT
DARK FRUIT
FRESH FRUIT

FLAVOR NOTES

SMELL / SCENT NOTES

OTHER NOTES

BOURBON NAME		DATE TASTED

PRODUCER	DISTILLERY

TYPE / GRADE	COUNTRY OF ORIGIN

STILL TYPE	REGION

AGE	ALCOHOL %	PRICE	BOTTLE SIZE

QUALITY RATING

1	2	3	4	5	6	7	8	9	10

VALUE FOR MONEY

1	2	3	4	5	6	7	8	9	10

COLOR METER

- BLACK
- DARK BROWN
- MAHOGANY
- BRICK
- DARK AMBER
- AMBER
- GOLD
- STRAW
- CLEAR

FLAVOR WHEEL

BALANCE, HEAT / ABM ____ %, FINISH, FRESH FRUIT, BODY, DARK FRUIT, PEATY / SMOKY, CITRUS FRUIT, SHARP / ACIDIC, DRIED FRUIT, ASTRINGENT, HERBAL / VEGETAL, ROASTED / WOODY, SPICES, MOLASSES, SWEET / CANDIED

FLAVOR NOTES

SMELL / SCENT NOTES

OTHER NOTES

BOURBON LOG

BOURBON NAME		DATE TASTED

PRODUCER	DISTILLERY

TYPE / GRADE	COUNTRY OF ORIGIN

STILL TYPE	REGION

AGE	ALCOHOL %	PRICE	BOTTLE SIZE

QUALITY RATING	VALUE FOR MONEY
1 2 3 4 5 6 7 8 9 10	1 2 3 4 5 6 7 8 9 10

COLOR METER

- BLACK
- DARK BROWN
- MAHOGANY
- BRICK
- DARK AMBER
- AMBER
- GOLD
- STRAW
- CLEAR

FLAVOR WHEEL

BALANCE
HEAT / ABM _____ %
FINISH
FRESH FRUIT
BODY
DARK FRUIT
PEATY / SMOKY
CITRUS FRUIT
SHARP / ACIDIC
DRIED FRUIT
ASTRINGENT
HERBAL / VEGETAL
ROASTED / WOODY
SPICES
MOLASSES
SWEET / CANDIED

FLAVOR NOTES

SMELL / SCENT NOTES	OTHER NOTES

BOURBON NAME		DATE TASTED

PRODUCER	DISTILLERY

TYPE / GRADE	COUNTRY OF ORIGIN

STILL TYPE	REGION

AGE	ALCOHOL %	PRICE	BOTTLE SIZE

QUALITY RATING

1	2	3	4	5	6	7	8	9	10

VALUE FOR MONEY

1	2	3	4	5	6	7	8	9	10

COLOR METER

- BLACK
- DARK BROWN
- MAHOGANY
- BRICK
- DARK AMBER
- AMBER
- GOLD
- STRAW
- CLEAR

FLAVOR WHEEL

BALANCE, FINISH, BODY, PEATY / SMOKY, SHARP / ACIDIC, ASTRINGENT, ROASTED / WOODY, MOLASSES, SWEET / CANDIED, SPICES, HERBAL / VEGETAL, DRIED FRUIT, CITRUS FRUIT, DARK FRUIT, FRESH FRUIT, HEAT / ABM _____ %

FLAVOR NOTES

SMELL / SCENT NOTES

OTHER NOTES

BOURBON LOG

BOURBON NAME	DATE TASTED

PRODUCER	DISTILLERY

TYPE / GRADE	COUNTRY OF ORIGIN

STILL TYPE	REGION

AGE	ALCOHOL %	PRICE	BOTTLE SIZE

QUALITY RATING

1	2	3	4	5	6	7	8	9	10

VALUE FOR MONEY

1	2	3	4	5	6	7	8	9	10

COLOR METER

- BLACK
- DARK BROWN
- MAHOGANY
- BRICK
- DARK AMBER
- AMBER
- GOLD
- STRAW
- CLEAR

FLAVOR WHEEL

BALANCE · HEAT / ABM _____ %
FINISH · FRESH FRUIT
BODY · DARK FRUIT
PEATY / SMOKY · CITRUS FRUIT
SHARP / ACIDIC · DRIED FRUIT
ASTRINGENT · HERBAL / VEGETAL
ROASTED / WOODY · SPICES
MOLASSES · SWEET / CANDIED

FLAVOR NOTES

SMELL / SCENT NOTES

OTHER NOTES

BOURBON NAME		DATE TASTED

PRODUCER	DISTILLERY

TYPE / GRADE	COUNTRY OF ORIGIN

STILL TYPE	REGION

AGE	ALCOHOL %	PRICE	BOTTLE SIZE

QUALITY RATING

1	2	3	4	5	6	7	8	9	10

VALUE FOR MONEY

1	2	3	4	5	6	7	8	9	10

COLOR METER

BLACK
DARK BROWN
MAHOGANY
BRICK
DARK AMBER
AMBER
GOLD
STRAW
CLEAR

FLAVOR WHEEL

BALANCE
HEAT / ABM _____ %
FINISH
FRESH FRUIT
BODY
PEATY / SMOKY
DARK FRUIT
SHARP / ACIDIC
CITRUS FRUIT
ASTRINGENT
DRIED FRUIT
ROASTED / WOODY
HERBAL / VEGETAL
MOLASSES
SPICES
SWEET / CANDIED

FLAVOR NOTES

SMELL / SCENT NOTES

OTHER NOTES

BOURBON LOG

BOURBON NAME		DATE TASTED

PRODUCER	DISTILLERY

TYPE / GRADE	COUNTRY OF ORIGIN

STILL TYPE	REGION

AGE	ALCOHOL %	PRICE	BOTTLE SIZE

QUALITY RATING

1	2	3	4	5	6	7	8	9	10

VALUE FOR MONEY

1	2	3	4	5	6	7	8	9	10

COLOR METER

- BLACK
- DARK BROWN
- MAHOGANY
- BRICK
- DARK AMBER
- AMBER
- GOLD
- STRAW
- CLEAR

FLAVOR WHEEL

HEAT / ABM _____ %

BALANCE
FINISH
BODY
PEATY / SMOKY
SHARP / ACIDIC
ASTRINGENT
ROASTED / WOODY
MOLASSES
SWEET / CANDIED
SPICES
HERBAL / VEGETAL
DRIED FRUIT
CITRUS FRUIT
DARK FRUIT
FRESH FRUIT

FLAVOR NOTES

SMELL / SCENT NOTES

OTHER NOTES

72

BOURBON NAME	DATE TASTED

PRODUCER	DISTILLERY

TYPE / GRADE	COUNTRY OF ORIGIN

STILL TYPE	REGION

AGE	ALCOHOL %	PRICE	BOTTLE SIZE

QUALITY RATING

1	2	3	4	5	6	7	8	9	10

VALUE FOR MONEY

1	2	3	4	5	6	7	8	9	10

COLOR METER

- BLACK
- DARK BROWN
- MAHOGANY
- BRICK
- DARK AMBER
- AMBER
- GOLD
- STRAW
- CLEAR

FLAVOR WHEEL

BALANCE, HEAT / ABM _____ %, FINISH, FRESH FRUIT, BODY, DARK FRUIT, PEATY / SMOKY, CITRUS FRUIT, SHARP / ACIDIC, DRIED FRUIT, ASTRINGENT, HERBAL / VEGETAL, ROASTED / WOODY, SPICES, MOLASSES, SWEET / CANDIED

FLAVOR NOTES

SMELL / SCENT NOTES

OTHER NOTES

BOURBON LOG

BOURBON NAME	DATE TASTED

PRODUCER	DISTILLERY

TYPE / GRADE	COUNTRY OF ORIGIN

STILL TYPE	REGION

AGE	ALCOHOL %	PRICE	BOTTLE SIZE

QUALITY RATING	VALUE FOR MONEY
1 2 3 4 5 6 7 8 9 10	1 2 3 4 5 6 7 8 9 10

COLOR METER

- BLACK
- DARK BROWN
- MAHOGANY
- BRICK
- DARK AMBER
- AMBER
- GOLD
- STRAW
- CLEAR

FLAVOR WHEEL

BALANCE   HEAT / ABM _____ %
FINISH
BODY
PEATY / SMOKY
SHARP / ACIDIC
ASTRINGENT
ROASTED / WOODY
MOLASSES
SWEET / CANDIED
SPICES
HERBAL / VEGETAL
DRIED FRUIT
CITRUS FRUIT
DARK FRUIT
FRESH FRUIT

FLAVOR NOTES

SMELL / SCENT NOTES

OTHER NOTES

BOURBON NAME		DATE TASTED

PRODUCER	DISTILLERY

TYPE / GRADE	COUNTRY OF ORIGIN

STILL TYPE	REGION

AGE	ALCOHOL %	PRICE	BOTTLE SIZE

QUALITY RATING

1	2	3	4	5	6	7	8	9	10

VALUE FOR MONEY

1	2	3	4	5	6	7	8	9	10

COLOR METER

- BLACK
- DARK BROWN
- MAHOGANY
- BRICK
- DARK AMBER
- AMBER
- GOLD
- STRAW
- CLEAR

FLAVOR WHEEL

BALANCE, HEAT / ABM _____ %, FINISH, FRESH FRUIT, BODY, DARK FRUIT, PEATY / SMOKY, CITRUS FRUIT, SHARP / ACIDIC, DRIED FRUIT, ASTRINGENT, HERBAL / VEGETAL, ROASTED / WOODY, SPICES, MOLASSES, SWEET / CANDIED

FLAVOR NOTES

SMELL / SCENT NOTES

OTHER NOTES

BOURBON LOG

BOURBON NAME	DATE TASTED

PRODUCER	DISTILLERY

TYPE / GRADE	COUNTRY OF ORIGIN

STILL TYPE	REGION

AGE	ALCOHOL %	PRICE	BOTTLE SIZE

QUALITY RATING

1	2	3	4	5	6	7	8	9	10

VALUE FOR MONEY

1	2	3	4	5	6	7	8	9	10

COLOR METER

- BLACK
- DARK BROWN
- MAHOGANY
- BRICK
- DARK AMBER
- AMBER
- GOLD
- STRAW
- CLEAR

FLAVOR WHEEL

HEAT / ABM _____ %

BALANCE
FINISH
BODY
PEATY / SMOKY
SHARP / ACIDIC
ASTRINGENT
ROASTED / WOODY
MOLASSES
SWEET / CANDIED
SPICES
HERBAL / VEGETAL
DRIED FRUIT
CITRUS FRUIT
DARK FRUIT
FRESH FRUIT

FLAVOR NOTES

SMELL / SCENT NOTES

OTHER NOTES

76

BOURBON NAME		DATE TASTED

PRODUCER	DISTILLERY

TYPE / GRADE	COUNTRY OF ORIGIN

STILL TYPE	REGION

AGE	ALCOHOL %	PRICE	BOTTLE SIZE

QUALITY RATING

1	2	3	4	5	6	7	8	9	10

VALUE FOR MONEY

1	2	3	4	5	6	7	8	9	10

COLOR METER

BLACK
DARK BROWN
MAHOGANY
BRICK
DARK AMBER
AMBER
GOLD
STRAW
CLEAR

FLAVOR WHEEL

HEAT / ABM _____ %
BALANCE
FINISH
BODY
FRESH FRUIT
PEATY / SMOKY
DARK FRUIT
SHARP / ACIDIC
CITRUS FRUIT
ASTRINGENT
DRIED FRUIT
ROASTED / WOODY
HERBAL / VEGETAL
MOLASSES
SPICES
SWEET / CANDIED

FLAVOR NOTES

SMELL / SCENT NOTES

OTHER NOTES

BOURBON LOG

BOURBON NAME	DATE TASTED

PRODUCER	DISTILLERY

TYPE / GRADE	COUNTRY OF ORIGIN

STILL TYPE	REGION

AGE	ALCOHOL %	PRICE	BOTTLE SIZE

QUALITY RATING

1	2	3	4	5	6	7	8	9	10

VALUE FOR MONEY

1	2	3	4	5	6	7	8	9	10

COLOR METER

- BLACK
- DARK BROWN
- MAHOGANY
- BRICK
- DARK AMBER
- AMBER
- GOLD
- STRAW
- CLEAR

FLAVOR WHEEL

BALANCE · HEAT / ABM _____ % · FINISH · FRESH FRUIT · BODY · DARK FRUIT · PEATY / SMOKY · CITRUS FRUIT · SHARP / ACIDIC · DRIED FRUIT · ASTRINGENT · HERBAL / VEGETAL · ROASTED / WOODY · SPICES · MOLASSES · SWEET / CANDIED

FLAVOR NOTES

SMELL / SCENT NOTES	OTHER NOTES

BOURBON NAME	DATE TASTED

PRODUCER	DISTILLERY

TYPE / GRADE	COUNTRY OF ORIGIN

STILL TYPE	REGION

AGE	ALCOHOL %	PRICE	BOTTLE SIZE

QUALITY RATING

1	2	3	4	5	6	7	8	9	10

VALUE FOR MONEY

1	2	3	4	5	6	7	8	9	10

COLOR METER

- BLACK
- DARK BROWN
- MAHOGANY
- BRICK
- DARK AMBER
- AMBER
- GOLD
- STRAW
- CLEAR

FLAVOR WHEEL

HEAT / ABM _____ %

BALANCE
FINISH
BODY
PEATY / SMOKY
SHARP / ACIDIC
ASTRINGENT
ROASTED / WOODY
MOLASSES
SWEET / CANDIED
SPICES
HERBAL / VEGETAL
DRIED FRUIT
CITRUS FRUIT
DARK FRUIT
FRESH FRUIT

FLAVOR NOTES

SMELL / SCENT NOTES

OTHER NOTES

BOURBON LOG

BOURBON NAME	DATE TASTED

PRODUCER	DISTILLERY

TYPE / GRADE	COUNTRY OF ORIGIN

STILL TYPE	REGION

AGE	ALCOHOL %	PRICE	BOTTLE SIZE

QUALITY RATING

1	2	3	4	5	6	7	8	9	10

VALUE FOR MONEY

1	2	3	4	5	6	7	8	9	10

COLOR METER

- BLACK
- DARK BROWN
- MAHOGANY
- BRICK
- DARK AMBER
- AMBER
- GOLD
- STRAW
- CLEAR

FLAVOR WHEEL

BALANCE — HEAT / ABM _____ %
FINISH
BODY
PEATY / SMOKY
SHARP / ACIDIC
ASTRINGENT
ROASTED / WOODY
MOLASSES
SWEET / CANDIED
SPICES
HERBAL / VEGETAL
DRIED FRUIT
CITRUS FRUIT
DARK FRUIT
FRESH FRUIT

FLAVOR NOTES

SMELL / SCENT NOTES

OTHER NOTES

BOURBON NAME		DATE TASTED

PRODUCER	DISTILLERY

TYPE / GRADE	COUNTRY OF ORIGIN

STILL TYPE	REGION

AGE	ALCOHOL %	PRICE	BOTTLE SIZE

QUALITY RATING

1	2	3	4	5	6	7	8	9	10

VALUE FOR MONEY

1	2	3	4	5	6	7	8	9	10

COLOR METER

- BLACK
- DARK BROWN
- MAHOGANY
- BRICK
- DARK AMBER
- AMBER
- GOLD
- STRAW
- CLEAR

FLAVOR WHEEL

HEAT / ABM _____ %

BALANCE, FINISH, BODY, PEATY / SMOKY, SHARP / ACIDIC, ASTRINGENT, ROASTED / WOODY, MOLASSES, SWEET / CANDIED, SPICES, HERBAL / VEGETAL, DRIED FRUIT, CITRUS FRUIT, DARK FRUIT, FRESH FRUIT

FLAVOR NOTES

SMELL / SCENT NOTES

OTHER NOTES

BOURBON LOG

BOURBON NAME		DATE TASTED

PRODUCER	DISTILLERY

TYPE / GRADE	COUNTRY OF ORIGIN

STILL TYPE	REGION

AGE	ALCOHOL %	PRICE	BOTTLE SIZE

QUALITY RATING

1	2	3	4	5	6	7	8	9	10

VALUE FOR MONEY

1	2	3	4	5	6	7	8	9	10

COLOR METER

- BLACK
- DARK BROWN
- MAHOGANY
- BRICK
- DARK AMBER
- AMBER
- GOLD
- STRAW
- CLEAR

FLAVOR WHEEL

BALANCE
FINISH
BODY
PEATY / SMOKY
SHARP / ACIDIC
ASTRINGENT
ROASTED / WOODY
MOLASSES
SWEET / CANDIED
SPICES
HERBAL / VEGETAL
DRIED FRUIT
CITRUS FRUIT
DARK FRUIT
FRESH FRUIT
HEAT / ABM _____ %

FLAVOR NOTES

SMELL / SCENT NOTES

OTHER NOTES

BOURBON NAME		DATE TASTED

PRODUCER	DISTILLERY

TYPE / GRADE	COUNTRY OF ORIGIN

STILL TYPE	REGION

AGE	ALCOHOL %	PRICE	BOTTLE SIZE

QUALITY RATING

1	2	3	4	5	6	7	8	9	10

VALUE FOR MONEY

1	2	3	4	5	6	7	8	9	10

COLOR METER

- BLACK
- DARK BROWN
- MAHOGANY
- BRICK
- DARK AMBER
- AMBER
- GOLD
- STRAW
- CLEAR

FLAVOR WHEEL

BALANCE · HEAT / ABM _____ % · FINISH · FRESH FRUIT · BODY · PEATY / SMOKY · DARK FRUIT · SHARP / ACIDIC · CITRUS FRUIT · ASTRINGENT · DRIED FRUIT · ROASTED / WOODY · HERBAL / VEGETAL · MOLASSES · SWEET / CANDIED · SPICES

FLAVOR NOTES

SMELL / SCENT NOTES

OTHER NOTES

BOURBON LOG

BOURBON NAME	DATE TASTED

PRODUCER	DISTILLERY

TYPE / GRADE	COUNTRY OF ORIGIN

STILL TYPE	REGION

AGE	ALCOHOL %	PRICE	BOTTLE SIZE

QUALITY RATING

1	2	3	4	5	6	7	8	9	10

VALUE FOR MONEY

1	2	3	4	5	6	7	8	9	10

COLOR METER

- BLACK
- DARK BROWN
- MAHOGANY
- BRICK
- DARK AMBER
- AMBER
- GOLD
- STRAW
- CLEAR

FLAVOR WHEEL

HEAT / ABM _____ %

BALANCE, FINISH, BODY, PEATY / SMOKY, SHARP / ACIDIC, ASTRINGENT, ROASTED / WOODY, MOLASSES, SWEET / CANDIED, SPICES, HERBAL / VEGETAL, DRIED FRUIT, CITRUS FRUIT, DARK FRUIT, FRESH FRUIT

FLAVOR NOTES

SMELL / SCENT NOTES

OTHER NOTES

BOURBON NAME		DATE TASTED

PRODUCER	DISTILLERY

TYPE / GRADE	COUNTRY OF ORIGIN

STILL TYPE	REGION

AGE	ALCOHOL %	PRICE	BOTTLE SIZE

QUALITY RATING

1	2	3	4	5	6	7	8	9	10

VALUE FOR MONEY

1	2	3	4	5	6	7	8	9	10

COLOR METER

- BLACK
- DARK BROWN
- MAHOGANY
- BRICK
- DARK AMBER
- AMBER
- GOLD
- STRAW
- CLEAR

FLAVOR WHEEL

HEAT / ABM _____ %

BALANCE
FINISH
BODY
PEATY / SMOKY
SHARP / ACIDIC
ASTRINGENT
ROASTED / WOODY
MOLASSES
SWEET / CANDIED
SPICES
HERBAL / VEGETAL
DRIED FRUIT
CITRUS FRUIT
DARK FRUIT
FRESH FRUIT

FLAVOR NOTES

SMELL / SCENT NOTES

OTHER NOTES

BOURBON LOG

BOURBON NAME	DATE TASTED

PRODUCER	DISTILLERY

TYPE / GRADE	COUNTRY OF ORIGIN

STILL TYPE	REGION

AGE	ALCOHOL %	PRICE	BOTTLE SIZE

QUALITY RATING	VALUE FOR MONEY
1 2 3 4 5 6 7 8 9 10	1 2 3 4 5 6 7 8 9 10

COLOR METER

- BLACK
- DARK BROWN
- MAHOGANY
- BRICK
- DARK AMBER
- AMBER
- GOLD
- STRAW
- CLEAR

FLAVOR WHEEL

BALANCE
FINISH
BODY
PEATY / SMOKY
SHARP / ACIDIC
ASTRINGENT
ROASTED / WOODY
MOLASSES
SWEET / CANDIED
SPICES
HERBAL / VEGETAL
DRIED FRUIT
CITRUS FRUIT
DARK FRUIT
FRESH FRUIT
HEAT / ABM _____ %

FLAVOR NOTES

SMELL / SCENT NOTES	OTHER NOTES

BOURBON NAME		DATE TASTED

PRODUCER	DISTILLERY

TYPE / GRADE	COUNTRY OF ORIGIN

STILL TYPE	REGION

AGE	ALCOHOL %	PRICE	BOTTLE SIZE

QUALITY RATING

1	2	3	4	5	6	7	8	9	10

VALUE FOR MONEY

1	2	3	4	5	6	7	8	9	10

COLOR METER

- BLACK
- DARK BROWN
- MAHOGANY
- BRICK
- DARK AMBER
- AMBER
- GOLD
- STRAW
- CLEAR

FLAVOR WHEEL

HEAT / ABM _____ %

BALANCE
FINISH
BODY
PEATY / SMOKY
SHARP / ACIDIC
ASTRINGENT
ROASTED / WOODY
MOLASSES
SWEET / CANDIED
SPICES
HERBAL / VEGETAL
DRIED FRUIT
CITRUS FRUIT
DARK FRUIT
FRESH FRUIT

FLAVOR NOTES

SMELL / SCENT NOTES

OTHER NOTES

BOURBON NAME		DATE TASTED

PRODUCER	DISTILLERY

TYPE / GRADE	COUNTRY OF ORIGIN

STILL TYPE	REGION

AGE	ALCOHOL %	PRICE	BOTTLE SIZE

QUALITY RATING

1	2	3	4	5	6	7	8	9	10

VALUE FOR MONEY

1	2	3	4	5	6	7	8	9	10

COLOR METER

- BLACK
- DARK BROWN
- MAHOGANY
- BRICK
- DARK AMBER
- AMBER
- GOLD
- STRAW
- CLEAR

FLAVOR WHEEL

HEAT / ABM _____ %

BALANCE
FINISH
BODY
PEATY / SMOKY
SHARP / ACIDIC
ASTRINGENT
ROASTED / WOODY
MOLASSES
SWEET / CANDIED
SPICES
HERBAL / VEGETAL
DRIED FRUIT
CITRUS FRUIT
DARK FRUIT
FRESH FRUIT

FLAVOR NOTES

SMELL / SCENT NOTES	OTHER NOTES

BOURBON NAME		DATE TASTED

PRODUCER	DISTILLERY

TYPE / GRADE	COUNTRY OF ORIGIN

STILL TYPE	REGION

AGE	ALCOHOL %	PRICE	BOTTLE SIZE

QUALITY RATING

1	2	3	4	5	6	7	8	9	10

VALUE FOR MONEY

1	2	3	4	5	6	7	8	9	10

COLOR METER

BLACK
DARK BROWN
MAHOGANY
BRICK
DARK AMBER
AMBER
GOLD
STRAW
CLEAR

FLAVOR WHEEL

HEAT / ABM _____ %
BALANCE
FINISH
BODY
FRESH FRUIT
PEATY / SMOKY
DARK FRUIT
SHARP / ACIDIC
CITRUS FRUIT
DRIED FRUIT
ASTRINGENT
ROASTED / WOODY
HERBAL / VEGETAL
MOLASSES
SPICES
SWEET / CANDIED

FLAVOR NOTES

SMELL / SCENT NOTES

OTHER NOTES

BOURBON LOG

BOURBON NAME	DATE TASTED

PRODUCER	DISTILLERY

TYPE / GRADE	COUNTRY OF ORIGIN

STILL TYPE	REGION

AGE	ALCOHOL %	PRICE	BOTTLE SIZE

QUALITY RATING

1	2	3	4	5	6	7	8	9	10

VALUE FOR MONEY

1	2	3	4	5	6	7	8	9	10

COLOR METER

- BLACK
- DARK BROWN
- MAHOGANY
- BRICK
- DARK AMBER
- AMBER
- GOLD
- STRAW
- CLEAR

FLAVOR WHEEL

HEAT / ABM _____ %

BALANCE, FINISH, BODY, PEATY / SMOKY, SHARP / ACIDIC, ASTRINGENT, ROASTED / WOODY, MOLASSES, SWEET / CANDIED, SPICES, HERBAL / VEGETAL, DRIED FRUIT, CITRUS FRUIT, DARK FRUIT, FRESH FRUIT

FLAVOR NOTES

SMELL / SCENT NOTES

OTHER NOTES

BOURBON NAME		DATE TASTED

PRODUCER	DISTILLERY

TYPE / GRADE	COUNTRY OF ORIGIN

STILL TYPE	REGION

AGE	ALCOHOL %	PRICE	BOTTLE SIZE

QUALITY RATING

1	2	3	4	5	6	7	8	9	10

VALUE FOR MONEY

1	2	3	4	5	6	7	8	9	10

COLOR METER

- BLACK
- DARK BROWN
- MAHOGANY
- BRICK
- DARK AMBER
- AMBER
- GOLD
- STRAW
- CLEAR

FLAVOR WHEEL

HEAT / ABM _____ %

BALANCE, FINISH, BODY, PEATY / SMOKY, SHARP / ACIDIC, ASTRINGENT, ROASTED / WOODY, MOLASSES, SWEET / CANDIED, SPICES, HERBAL / VEGETAL, DRIED FRUIT, CITRUS FRUIT, DARK FRUIT, FRESH FRUIT

FLAVOR NOTES

SMELL / SCENT NOTES

OTHER NOTES

BOURBON LOG

BOURBON NAME		DATE TASTED

PRODUCER	DISTILLERY

TYPE / GRADE	COUNTRY OF ORIGIN

STILL TYPE	REGION

AGE	ALCOHOL %	PRICE	BOTTLE SIZE

QUALITY RATING

1	2	3	4	5	6	7	8	9	10

VALUE FOR MONEY

1	2	3	4	5	6	7	8	9	10

COLOR METER

- BLACK
- DARK BROWN
- MAHOGANY
- BRICK
- DARK AMBER
- AMBER
- GOLD
- STRAW
- CLEAR

FLAVOR WHEEL

BALANCE · HEAT / ABM _____ %
FINISH · FRESH FRUIT
BODY · DARK FRUIT
PEATY / SMOKY · CITRUS FRUIT
SHARP / ACIDIC · DRIED FRUIT
ASTRINGENT · HERBAL / VEGETAL
ROASTED / WOODY · SPICES
MOLASSES · SWEET / CANDIED

FLAVOR NOTES

SMELL / SCENT NOTES

OTHER NOTES

BOURBON NAME		DATE TASTED

PRODUCER	DISTILLERY

TYPE / GRADE	COUNTRY OF ORIGIN

STILL TYPE	REGION

AGE	ALCOHOL %	PRICE	BOTTLE SIZE

QUALITY RATING

1	2	3	4	5	6	7	8	9	10

VALUE FOR MONEY

1	2	3	4	5	6	7	8	9	10

COLOR METER

- BLACK
- DARK BROWN
- MAHOGANY
- BRICK
- DARK AMBER
- AMBER
- GOLD
- STRAW
- CLEAR

FLAVOR WHEEL

HEAT / ABM _____ %

BALANCE, FINISH, BODY, PEATY / SMOKY, SHARP / ACIDIC, ASTRINGENT, ROASTED / WOODY, MOLASSES, SWEET / CANDIED, SPICES, HERBAL / VEGETAL, DRIED FRUIT, CITRUS FRUIT, DARK FRUIT, FRESH FRUIT

FLAVOR NOTES

SMELL / SCENT NOTES

OTHER NOTES

BOURBON LOG

BOURBON NAME		DATE TASTED

PRODUCER	DISTILLERY

TYPE / GRADE	COUNTRY OF ORIGIN

STILL TYPE	REGION

AGE	ALCOHOL %	PRICE	BOTTLE SIZE

QUALITY RATING

1	2	3	4	5	6	7	8	9	10

VALUE FOR MONEY

1	2	3	4	5	6	7	8	9	10

COLOR METER

- BLACK
- DARK BROWN
- MAHOGANY
- BRICK
- DARK AMBER
- AMBER
- GOLD
- STRAW
- CLEAR

FLAVOR WHEEL

BALANCE
HEAT / ABM _____ %
FINISH
FRESH FRUIT
BODY
PEATY / SMOKY
DARK FRUIT
SHARP / ACIDIC
CITRUS FRUIT
ASTRINGENT
DRIED FRUIT
ROASTED / WOODY
HERBAL / VEGETAL
MOLASSES
SPICES
SWEET / CANDIED

FLAVOR NOTES

SMELL / SCENT NOTES

OTHER NOTES

BOURBON NAME		DATE TASTED

PRODUCER	DISTILLERY

TYPE / GRADE	COUNTRY OF ORIGIN

STILL TYPE	REGION

AGE	ALCOHOL %	PRICE	BOTTLE SIZE

QUALITY RATING

1	2	3	4	5	6	7	8	9	10

VALUE FOR MONEY

1	2	3	4	5	6	7	8	9	10

COLOR METER

- BLACK
- DARK BROWN
- MAHOGANY
- BRICK
- DARK AMBER
- AMBER
- GOLD
- STRAW
- CLEAR

FLAVOR WHEEL

HEAT / ABM _____ %

BALANCE, FINISH, BODY, PEATY / SMOKY, SHARP / ACIDIC, ASTRINGENT, ROASTED / WOODY, MOLASSES, SWEET / CANDIED, SPICES, HERBAL / VEGETAL, DRIED FRUIT, CITRUS FRUIT, DARK FRUIT, FRESH FRUIT

FLAVOR NOTES

SMELL / SCENT NOTES

OTHER NOTES

BOURBON LOG

BOURBON NAME		DATE TASTED

PRODUCER	DISTILLERY

TYPE / GRADE	COUNTRY OF ORIGIN

STILL TYPE	REGION

AGE	ALCOHOL %	PRICE	BOTTLE SIZE

QUALITY RATING

1	2	3	4	5	6	7	8	9	10

VALUE FOR MONEY

1	2	3	4	5	6	7	8	9	10

COLOR METER

- BLACK
- DARK BROWN
- MAHOGANY
- BRICK
- DARK AMBER
- AMBER
- GOLD
- STRAW
- CLEAR

FLAVOR WHEEL

HEAT / ABM _____ %

BALANCE
FINISH
BODY
PEATY / SMOKY
SHARP / ACIDIC
ASTRINGENT
ROASTED / WOODY
MOLASSES
SWEET / CANDIED
SPICES
HERBAL / VEGETAL
DRIED FRUIT
CITRUS FRUIT
DARK FRUIT
FRESH FRUIT

FLAVOR NOTES

SMELL / SCENT NOTES

OTHER NOTES

BOURBON NAME	DATE TASTED

PRODUCER	DISTILLERY

TYPE / GRADE	COUNTRY OF ORIGIN

STILL TYPE	REGION

AGE	ALCOHOL %	PRICE	BOTTLE SIZE

QUALITY RATING

1	2	3	4	5	6	7	8	9	10

VALUE FOR MONEY

1	2	3	4	5	6	7	8	9	10

COLOR METER

BLACK
DARK BROWN
MAHOGANY
BRICK
DARK AMBER
AMBER
GOLD
STRAW
CLEAR

FLAVOR WHEEL

BALANCE, HEAT / ABM _____ %, FINISH, BODY, PEATY / SMOKY, SHARP / ACIDIC, ASTRINGENT, ROASTED / WOODY, MOLASSES, SWEET / CANDIED, SPICES, HERBAL / VEGETAL, DRIED FRUIT, CITRUS FRUIT, DARK FRUIT, FRESH FRUIT

FLAVOR NOTES

SMELL / SCENT NOTES

OTHER NOTES

BOURBON LOG

BOURBON NAME	DATE TASTED

PRODUCER	DISTILLERY

TYPE / GRADE	COUNTRY OF ORIGIN

STILL TYPE	REGION

AGE	ALCOHOL %	PRICE	BOTTLE SIZE

QUALITY RATING

1	2	3	4	5	6	7	8	9	10

VALUE FOR MONEY

1	2	3	4	5	6	7	8	9	10

COLOR METER

- BLACK
- DARK BROWN
- MAHOGANY
- BRICK
- DARK AMBER
- AMBER
- GOLD
- STRAW
- CLEAR

FLAVOR WHEEL

BALANCE · HEAT / ABM _____ % · FINISH · BODY · FRESH FRUIT · PEATY / SMOKY · DARK FRUIT · SHARP / ACIDIC · CITRUS FRUIT · ASTRINGENT · DRIED FRUIT · ROASTED / WOODY · HERBAL / VEGETAL · MOLASSES · SPICES · SWEET / CANDIED

FLAVOR NOTES

SMELL / SCENT NOTES

OTHER NOTES

BOURBON NAME	DATE TASTED

PRODUCER	DISTILLERY

TYPE / GRADE	COUNTRY OF ORIGIN

STILL TYPE	REGION

AGE	ALCOHOL %	PRICE	BOTTLE SIZE

QUALITY RATING

1	2	3	4	5	6	7	8	9	10

VALUE FOR MONEY

1	2	3	4	5	6	7	8	9	10

COLOR METER

BLACK
DARK BROWN
MAHOGANY
BRICK
DARK AMBER
AMBER
GOLD
STRAW
CLEAR

FLAVOR WHEEL

BALANCE, FINISH, BODY, PEATY / SMOKY, SHARP / ACIDIC, ASTRINGENT, ROASTED / WOODY, MOLASSES, SWEET / CANDIED, SPICES, HERBAL / VEGETAL, DRIED FRUIT, CITRUS FRUIT, DARK FRUIT, FRESH FRUIT, HEAT / ABM _____ %

FLAVOR NOTES

SMELL / SCENT NOTES

OTHER NOTES

BOURBON LOG

BOURBON NAME	DATE TASTED

PRODUCER	DISTILLERY

TYPE / GRADE	COUNTRY OF ORIGIN

STILL TYPE	REGION

AGE	ALCOHOL %	PRICE	BOTTLE SIZE

QUALITY RATING

1	2	3	4	5	6	7	8	9	10

VALUE FOR MONEY

1	2	3	4	5	6	7	8	9	10

COLOR METER

- BLACK
- DARK BROWN
- MAHOGANY
- BRICK
- DARK AMBER
- AMBER
- GOLD
- STRAW
- CLEAR

FLAVOR WHEEL

BALANCE
HEAT / ABM _____ %
FINISH
FRESH FRUIT
BODY
PEATY / SMOKY
DARK FRUIT
SHARP / ACIDIC
CITRUS FRUIT
ASTRINGENT
DRIED FRUIT
ROASTED / WOODY
HERBAL / VEGETAL
MOLASSES
SPICES
SWEET / CANDIED

FLAVOR NOTES

SMELL / SCENT NOTES

OTHER NOTES

BOURBON NAME

DATE TASTED

PRODUCER

DISTILLERY

TYPE / GRADE

COUNTRY OF ORIGIN

STILL TYPE

REGION

AGE	ALCOHOL %	PRICE	BOTTLE SIZE

QUALITY RATING

1	2	3	4	5	6	7	8	9	10

VALUE FOR MONEY

1	2	3	4	5	6	7	8	9	10

COLOR METER

BLACK
DARK BROWN
MAHOGANY
BRICK
DARK AMBER
AMBER
GOLD
STRAW
CLEAR

FLAVOR WHEEL

BALANCE, HEAT / ABM ____ %, FINISH, FRESH FRUIT, BODY, DARK FRUIT, PEATY / SMOKY, CITRUS FRUIT, SHARP / ACIDIC, DRIED FRUIT, ASTRINGENT, HERBAL / VEGETAL, ROASTED / WOODY, SPICES, MOLASSES, SWEET / CANDIED

FLAVOR NOTES

SMELL / SCENT NOTES

OTHER NOTES

BOURBON LOG

BOURBON NAME	DATE TASTED

PRODUCER	DISTILLERY

TYPE / GRADE	COUNTRY OF ORIGIN

STILL TYPE	REGION

AGE	ALCOHOL %	PRICE	BOTTLE SIZE

QUALITY RATING

1	2	3	4	5	6	7	8	9	10

VALUE FOR MONEY

1	2	3	4	5	6	7	8	9	10

COLOR METER

- BLACK
- DARK BROWN
- MAHOGANY
- BRICK
- DARK AMBER
- AMBER
- GOLD
- STRAW
- CLEAR

FLAVOR WHEEL

BALANCE
HEAT / ABM _____ %
FINISH
FRESH FRUIT
BODY
DARK FRUIT
PEATY / SMOKY
CITRUS FRUIT
SHARP / ACIDIC
ASTRINGENT
DRIED FRUIT
ROASTED / WOODY
HERBAL / VEGETAL
MOLASSES
SPICES
SWEET / CANDIED

FLAVOR NOTES

SMELL / SCENT NOTES	OTHER NOTES

BOURBON NAME		DATE TASTED

PRODUCER	DISTILLERY

TYPE / GRADE	COUNTRY OF ORIGIN

STILL TYPE	REGION

AGE	ALCOHOL %	PRICE	BOTTLE SIZE

QUALITY RATING

1	2	3	4	5	6	7	8	9	10

VALUE FOR MONEY

1	2	3	4	5	6	7	8	9	10

COLOR METER

BLACK
DARK BROWN
MAHOGANY
BRICK
DARK AMBER
AMBER
GOLD
STRAW
CLEAR

FLAVOR WHEEL

HEAT / ABM _____ %
BALANCE, FINISH, BODY, PEATY / SMOKY, SHARP / ACIDIC, ASTRINGENT, ROASTED / WOODY, MOLASSES, SWEET / CANDIED, SPICES, HERBAL / VEGETAL, DRIED FRUIT, CITRUS FRUIT, DARK FRUIT, FRESH FRUIT

FLAVOR NOTES

SMELL / SCENT NOTES

OTHER NOTES

NOTES

NOTES

THANKYOU FOR YOUR PURCHASE!

If you get the chance, please consider leaving
an honest review on Amazon. We appreciate
every one

Made in United States
Troutdale, OR
12/22/2024

27192395R00070